She "s
Knows God Loves
you.... warts & All !

Chm John

Jer. 29:11

"Women are very comfortable telling their hairdressers much more than a hairdresser ever wants to know. They arrive at the beauty salon with questions. Cherie's book gives the answers."

—Florence Littauer, International Speaker and Author, Founder of CLASS

"*Honest, Heartfelt,* and *Healing* are three words I would use to describe Cherie Jobe's powerful book, *Secrets from Behind the Chair.* Cherie uses her years of experience as a hairstylist to bring us life lessons that lead us to the Savior. You will find comfort for your soul and strength for your journey through the words and stories in this book."

—Karol Ladd, Author of *The Power of a Positive Woman*

"Cherie Jobe has proven to be a thoughtful listener to the words and hearts of people and a faithful recorder of their stories. Stories are both therapeutic to the teller and a witness to those who hear them. This book demonstrates the sensitivity Cherie has for a person's feelings and their need to share their journey of faith. The pages record the battles and victories God has provided to persons like you and me."

—Patsy Highland, Ph.D., Licensed Professional Counselor, Author of *Marriage Counseling 101 for Ministers*

"Reading *Secrets from Behind the Chair* will be a beauty make-over for your soul. Cherie's candid insights are expressed in such a creative manner that you are smiling as your soul is filling up with hope!"

—Jackie Kendall, Best-Selling Author of *Lady in Waiting*, President of Power to Grow, Inc.

"I was blessed to walk with Cherie as her relationship with God moved eighteen inches from her head to her heart. She began to walk with God every moment of her life. Her passion to share how Christ changed her life reminds me of the woman at the well in John 4. She writes from a life experience and does not hesitate to reveal her past hurts and pain. By sharing where she was before Christ, Cherie helps others see where they can be in their relationship with Christ. When she writes about 'Forgiven and Set Free,' what else can be said? *Secrets from Behind the Chair* is a message of hope written by a woman who understands what it means to be living with hope."

—Phillip C. Barnett, D.Min., Pastor, Cornerstone Baptist Church, KY

SECRETS
from Behind the
CHAIR

Secrets
from Behind the
Chair

WWW.CHERIEJOBE.COM

ISBN: 978-1-935786-62-7

Printed in the United States of America

St. Clair Publications

To all of the women who bear the burden of a secret
And to Jim, who loves me in spite of mine

Contents

Introduction

Over the thirty years that I've served as a hairdresser, my hands have been in the hair of quite a number of people. It took me many years to truly understand Minnie Pearl's famous statement, "Beauty is only skin deep."

Through my own trials and tribulations, I've been able to relate to pretty much every secret situation my clients could throw at me, and as a result, I've spent a lifetime counseling from "behind the chair." While I worked on the outside beauty, I was struggling with my own inner beauty, as well as the inner beauty of my clients.

I have completely embraced the concept from the Bible that God works in mysterious ways. He spoke to me on a beach through broken seashells, which has nothing to do with permanents or the latest craze in haircuts. God placed in my heart a book about broken hearts and lives just like all of the broken shells on the beach. I have taken the brokenness of my own life and thirty years of listening and counseling from behind the chair and used those experiences to share God's love and grace through my clients.

By now you're probably thinking about all the counseling/hair sessions you have had with someone else's hands in your hair. You may have experienced rejection, shame, and abuse and shared some of those innermost secrets with your hairdresser. Your life may have been touched by a person you came to know and trust from "behind the chair." Either way, I hope that these stories find connections with your own, allowing you to find some comfort as you sit in my chair.

My prayer for you is that your life is changed by the forgiveness and redeeming love of a God who is always at your side no matter what course your life will take. If you have never experienced that love and forgiveness, I hope this book will get into your hair and into your heart and change your life.

Before we can start, I really must get you on my appointment calendar! And don't be late because I want you to be more beautiful and transformed from within your own heart.

A Note from Behind the Chair

Over the years, my clients and I have built strong relationships on shared trust, honesty, and support. I value the trust that each client has given me, so I feel the need to tell you that I have been given permission to share their personal stories with you. Their names have been changed to protect their personal identity.

I want to thank each person who has bravely shared his or her own personal God story. Together, we give Him all the glory for putting our lives back together again.

We hope that, through these stories, you'll trust Him to do the same.

In His love,
Cherie

Chapter 1

Secrets of the Unloved

E ach of us has a story to tell that has been shaped by our unique histories and personalities. As we go through life, our individual lives intertwine, and other stories impact our own. Naturally, my mother's story impacted me a great deal, and at first, not so much in a good way.

My mother conceived me during her senior year in high school, so right from the start, I was blamed by family members for ruining her life. Words were whispered in secret, and suggestions were made for Mother to end her pregnancy. Thank goodness, she declined those suggestions, and she and my dad married on March 24, 1956.

Once I arrived, both sets of grandparents simply adored me. But during my adolescent years, I began hearing that same message. My mother was always making comments to friends that no one had really wanted me since I had been conceived out of wedlock. Hearing this repeated throughout my young life made quite an impression on a girl's mind. So guess what I came to believe about myself? Those feelings of being unloved from birth followed me wherever I went, because they lived inside me.

Do thoughts of "Nobody loves me" haunt you too?

I started playing competitive sports at a very young age. Looking back now, I realize the connection with my own mother's love for these sports, and I believe I worked so hard at them as another way for me to earn her love and acceptance.

{ Do thoughts of "Nobody loves me" haunt you too? }

When she watched me play, I felt so valued and important—that is, as long as I excelled. From those early experiences I learned that love was something I could earn. Since I was never rooted and grounded in unconditional love, I could never be relaxed or confident because I knew my acceptance was based on my performance or my perfect behavior.

My daddy, whom I loved so much, never came to watch me play. I found out later that he would brag about me and my sports abilities to his buddies. It was wonderful to discover in my thirties that my daddy had been proud of me, but how much would my sense of worth have been affected if I had known how my daddy felt about me then, when I was young and impressionable? It would have been life-changing for me.

God created little girls and women to be loved and cherished. When we don't know in the core of our being that we are precious and valued, we often seek outside approval. A child with an empty emotional tank will do anything to get attention, even if the only attention comes in the form of spanking or yelling.

Sometimes when grown men and women feel lonely, abandoned, and unloved, they desperately try anything to stop the pain. We start shoveling to fill the empty hole inside us, without stopping to think about the consequences of what we are doing, or how it will devastate those we love. At the time, we don't realize or want to admit that the choices we are making are self-sabotaging acts that will plunge us deeper into our dark hole. I know—because I did it all!

Saturday, 9:00 a.m. - Lucy

Listening to Lucy is much like eating a Tootsie Pop, along with the excitement you get when you reach the center. With every appointment, she has another life event to share. She's a teacher, and we often find ourselves talking about how some children are disrespectful and lazy these days. Most of the time we just laugh about how clumsy and stiff we are getting. Still, she always seems to greet life's roadblocks with a smile.

I have to confess, when I was asked to share my story, my heart immediately started to race. Not because of excitement, but because of the fear that I would have to take off my mask and share the truth about my life.

I basically grew up an average American girl from Huntsville, Alabama. We lived in a modest neighborhood, and as an only child, I spent lots of time playing outside with my imaginary friend. My father was never at home a lot, which made me always wonder how my parents could fight and argue so much. Being the only child of an overly protective mother, I always looked forward to going to my cousins' house.

As a child I always loved sports. Of all the sports I played I had a passion for volleyball. I felt the excitement in every play. Running up and down the court gave me such freedom from the real world. Eventually everyone outgrew me, so I became the manager for the team; elementary and high school years just flew by. I woke up one day, and it was time for college.

College was the beginning of a new life. In high school I dated this guy for almost all four years. We broke up right before I started college. The first week of college I met a boy I thought was gorgeous, smart, and funny all rolled into one. Life was good!

For three and a half years, Tim and I dated. There were red flags in this relationship, but I chose to ignore them. You know, girls, we believe we can change anything that's wrong with our man. I had waited for twenty-two years to marry. I knew this was the guy God had made for me. So we married in 1982. After we both graduated, we moved to Athens, Georgia. Life was very turbulent; we fought about everything. We didn't realize how different we were until I found out he wanted crunchy peanut butter, I wanted smooth; he wanted his jeans pressed, and I wanted mine folded. It was crazy!

We had our first child in 1987, and we moved into our first home the same year. Our second child came in 1989, and I thought our life together was absolutely wonderful. The key word here is "I." Tim's job began to take him away from home a lot. He was the athletic director and coach for his school. I began noticing that he was leaving the house for strange reasons. He would go out for donuts or to the store at strange hours. Later I found out he had become addicted to pornography. His strange behavior was because he was either taking back or picking up movies. I had no clue this was going on!

While trying to keep our marriage together, we became very involved in church. Tim's mother died in 1991, so I thought he might want to move back to Tennessee to be with his father. He wasn't very interested, which seemed strange to me. Later I learned that he was having an affair with a woman at work. He had been talking to her during his mother's illness because she had lost her mother, and she understood him more than I could. No wonder he didn't want to move!

Our third child came in 1992, followed by our fourth child in 1997. I remember so well thinking, "How could this be happening to me?" Emotionally, I checked out after finding out about the affair.

Now having four children, I decided it was time for me to forgive Tim and see if we could get back to the point when we first met, sharing with each other, being constant companions—the way things are when you're first in love. When I told him my thoughts about working on our marriage, he surprisingly said he didn't want to work on it.

In February 2005, I learned why he wasn't interested in working on the marriage. As I was doing some household cleaning one day, I came upon some letters. Much to my surprise I didn't recognize any of the content. They were filled with passion and excitement, something I had not felt in a long time. I knew at that moment, those words were not addressed to me. I confronted him later that evening, and he confessed to all the affairs, many I never knew of. Looking back on my life with Tim, I now can see the signs of betrayal. He never wanted me to go places with him, he was always up late at night on the computer, he was very secretive of his personal belongings, and there were many, many unexplained absences. After many long nights, waiting and crying out to God for direction about what to do, we finally divorced in 2007.

This experience has been the most heart-wrenching thing I have ever gone through. With that said, I believe there are many women who are walking down similar roads. I want those women to know that my strength to endure such pain has come only through my faith in Jesus Christ. In the days when loneliness was my constant companion, I remembered God's great promise to me in Hebrews 13:5: "Never will I leave you; never will I forsake you." I believe that no matter how painful or difficult my situation is, God is always there. I know I can look to Him for deliverance when I commit any situation to His care.

Tuesday, 2:00 p.m. – Rachel

The frailty of her body, the scars on her face, and the thinness of her hair reflect the pain hidden deep inside Rachel's heart, a pain that has also made her wise beyond her years.

I grew up in a small Tennessee town. I was not an only child, but it seemed as if I were. My three older sisters left home at early ages. My mother worked hard all her life in factories. She was a caretaker and a pleaser, so I did very little at home. Mom did it all—which sounds great, but when I got older, I didn't know how to do anything and didn't really want to do much.

My dad was an alcoholic but a hard-working man. His weekend binges would result in Mother, usually accompanied by me, looking for him in beer joints and begging him to come home. He'd be happy at first; then he'd get mean and verbally abusive to my mother. We all knew he had a problem, but it was "hush hush." Neither of my parents showed me much affection. I think that's why I crave attention today . . . especially from men.

I think my depression actually began in childhood and still continues today. I cried a lot, frequently misbehaved, stayed angry, and often told my parents I hated them. I wanted a happy home just as all other children had. Their answer to my cry for love was to give me money or anything I wanted. That has messed me up all my life.

At fifteen, I was drinking, smoking pot, and popping pills—always something. I never thought I had a problem; I just found ways to ease the pain. I didn't have anyone giving me the love I craved so I sought to feel good through alcohol and drugs.

I married at eighteen, and we based our marriage

on partying and having a good time. The cocaine made me numb. I didn't want to feel anything. We stayed married for fifteen years, and I thought it was a fairly good life. When I look back now, our life was out of control.

We had a daughter, Allison. Though I stopped the drugs while pregnant, I went straight back after she was born. I wasn't going to stop doing what I was doing, but I knew I could get her out of that life. So I gave my sister custody, and today she is a wonderful, smart, and athletic teenager with a lot going for her. I am so proud of her. This was the best decision I ever made. Allison has the love and confidence that I have never felt.

My second daughter, May, was born with drugs in her system. She lived only nine days. Her brain damage could have been from a high fever I had during pregnancy, but it was automatically assumed to be the result of my cocaine use. After her death, I was charged with reckless homicide and spent three years in jail. Jail was awful. Thankfully, I took my Bible with me. It is a shame that we have to get to our lowest point to turn to Him, but maybe He gets us there for a reason.

In prison I was forced to quit the drugs, and I felt

better than I had in my entire life. I went to church and could see God working in my life every day as I interacted with others in jail. I am so thankful for that time. But as soon as I got out of jail, I went right back to drugs. This time it was a straight downhill slide. I was soon arrested again.

Somehow I have ended up at the Blue Monarch. I am not sure how I was able to come here since there is a huge waiting list. Once again, God had His hand on me. Blue Monarch is a nonprofit organization designed to serve oppressed and abused women and their children who are currently recovering from abuses, addictions, or family issues. Each woman is offered a one-year residential program designed to fit her individual needs. Boy, was I needing a new design!

While housed here, women may further their education, break addictions, and even obtain a job. The goal is to give women hope for themselves and their children and equip them with the tools to become strong, confident, and self-sufficient.

I feel like my heart is getting filled. I don't hurt like I did. I have felt more love than ever. The most important thing I have learned during this difficult time is that the One who allows the difficulty is the One who loves me more than anyone else in the whole universe.

{ STRANDS of HOPE }

. . . .

Give thanks to the LORD, for he is good;
his love endures forever.

–PSALM 107:1

. . . .

Read that again: *forever.*

There are so many circumstances that life can throw at us to leave us feeling unloved. If we allow imperfect humans to shape our lives, we end up broken and unfulfilled. But filling our hearts and lives with the healing, unconditional love of a perfect, infinite God will allow His light to shine through our lives of darkness and despair.

Think About It

- When in your life have you ever felt unloved?

- Was there a certain person or persons who made you feel that way?

- Looking through the eyes of that person, can you see a reason why they may have behaved in that way?

- Take time now to forgive that person or persons for the ways in which they hurt you. If possible and appropriate, let the person know that you have forgiven him or her.

- Spend some time in truth, learning what the Bible tells you about love.

Pray About It

Loving and caring Father, please bring truth
to any lies that the enemy may have told me
about true godly love.

Overflow my heart with a love that is unconditional and real. I want to feel love and give
love the way Jesus does.

Validate my purpose and help me to use
my gifts and talents to bring glory to Your
name.

Educate me with the truth hidden in Your
Word. I need to understand together with
all the saints how deep, wide, and high the
love of God really is.

Drive me into the harbor of Your love, so that
I can find assurance, hope, rest, and safety in
Your amazing love.

Amen

Chapter 2

Secrets of the Innocent

A s the Serenity Prayer says: God, grant me the serenity to accept the things I cannot change, the courage to change the things I can, and the wisdom to know the difference.

At age six, going to Grandmother's house should be full of pleasant memories, like playing in the backyard on my swing set or decorating cookies at her kitchen table. One of my fondest memories was playing with all the dogs and cats she had running around. Granny was known for housing all the stray animals that needed a home.

One morning Mother needed to drop off my brother and me at Granny's for her to babysit. She lived out in the country, and on this particular morning, Granny had gone to town before we had arrived. With both hands full of two little ones, Mother stood on the small white porch waiting for her to come to the door.

When the door opened, my uncle stood framed in the doorway. "Where's Granny?" asked Mother.

"She had to run into town for a little while," my uncle explained.

"Well, I need a baby sitter for these two," Mother answered.

Strangely my uncle said he would be glad to watch one of us, but not two. Since I was the oldest, my mother decided to leave me. She knew I wouldn't cause as much trouble as my brother. Leaving her daughter with a family member wasn't something that seemed so out of the ordinary. My uncle played with me outside, pushed me on the swing, and played Mother May I, my favorite game, until I was exhausted. We came inside and ate lunch, and as usual, I laid down for a nap. My uncle said he was tired also and lay down beside me.

Cuddling was something that my daddy did often with

me, but my uncle wasn't touching me the same way. His hands and body parts were doing something a six-year-old did not understand. "Don't ever tell anyone," whispered silently in my young mind. But those whispers didn't take on meaning until years later when I came to understand what had happened on the visit to my grandmother's house.

When I told Mother what had happened, she told me that I wasn't telling the truth. My uncle wouldn't do such a thing. She confronted him and chose to believe him rather than me. She never realized how deeply her betrayal hurt me.

Friday, 10:00 a.m. – Carol

Carol is an attractive young lady with beautiful auburn hair. She loves animals; they love her unconditionally. As she learned to trust me to make her beautiful on the outside, she also shared bits of her "ugly" inside.

My mother was very abusive both physically and verbally. I was told from the earliest memory that I was never wanted and that she wished that I had never been born. She burned me with curling irons, ripped the hair out of my head, and cut me with knives. She ripped up pictures and made it impossible for me to maintain friendships by being rude and insulting in front of my few friends. She would always embarrass me in public by making fun of me, calling me a slut, and hitting me. Sometimes she would listen to my phone conversations through the vents in the garage. Mother had no friends and was jealous if I had some. I never understood why she mistreated me.

My mother drummed into my head that there was no God or angels; there were only UFOs and aliens. Kids made fun of me when I would tell them my family didn't go to church and believed in UFOs. I never saw a Bible as a child, just UFO books and magazines. When I did sleep, I would make up an escape, where I would touch the scar on my left wrist (most likely came from a burn from my mother) and be able to go home to my true alien family in the sky. I truly believed that this family existed and they were loving and kind.

My mother was lazy! I would clean the house on the weekends after going to school all week, while she lay on the couch all day and watch her taped soap operas. I became a neat freak and a full-time housekeeper as early as I can remember.

We had a weight machine in the basement. While

living at home in that hell, it provided another escape. It helped me to get physically strong as my mother got worse. I thought if I was stronger, then nobody would bully me.

One night I wasn't strong enough for a boy named Chester. We went to a concert, and afterward he raped me. I am so thankful I was on my period, and I didn't get pregnant.

My parents were into having "stuff." Televisions were in every room, so she could watch her soaps. Going on a vacation meant going to an Ethan Allen Store to buy furniture or just look around. My dad still has the same furniture and still feels that he has to show off his "stuff" that he worked for. I never saw my parents help anyone, not even me. I was given nothing when my mother died. I asked for a keyboard for my son, since he wanted to learn to play. She's now dead, and her keyboard sits rotting in the house with no one playing it.

My ex-husband of fourteen years was a horrific man. He had an affair for eight years while we were still married. He's now in prison for a devastating crime to a child. He changed from a nice guy to a totally self-absorbed stranger once I delivered our first child.

The abuse from my parents continued long into

my adult life. During my divorce trial, my parents supported my ex and testified against me since I was no
longer letting them see the grandchildren. I didn't want
my children exposed to the same hostile environment
that I had grown up in. That day I lost my husband and
my parents, and my children suffered even more.

The first guy I dated after my divorce cheated on
me. I was truly in love with him. I even introduced him
to my children, and then I was crushed again when he
left me.

I had my first love find me after eighteen years. He
wanted me and my sons to live with him, out of state,
and in his house. He was still married but stated that
he loved me, and we were what he always wanted.
Much to my surprise, I didn't do that foolish thing! Yes,
it was flattering but not real.

People change and, as romantic as it sounds, I want
a real relationship, not just to shack up with someone.
I've learned to stand my ground for Jesus and my
values.

The last words my mother ever told me: "You know
what you can do with your Jesus." But I thank Jesus
every day for the positive influence of my grandfather
who prayed for me his entire life. I was there with him
when he died on February 14, 1991. He died knowing

that I was saved and I had a personal relationship with my heavenly Father. Even though I have felt the pain of betrayal from my family, I know the Bible says in Hebrews 13:5 that Jesus will never leave nor forsake me. God is the only one who can give you light and sustain you during times of depression, discouragement, uncertainty, and fear.

If you are confronted with painful circumstances today, don't be afraid. Recognize that God is your Shepherd, your Father, your Friend. He will not forsake you.

Friday, 4:00 p.m. - Dana

School teacher by day and beauty consultant by night, this woman is a knockout! Her highlighted blonde hair reflects her bubbly personality. But underneath the mask of beauty and confidence, she, too, hides the sting of abuse.

My parents were divorced when I was not quite six months old. Mother left Daddy to raise four kids by himself. She had an affair with a man she ended up marrying.

We were all close to Daddy. He worked very hard, was a strong disciplinarian, and not demonstrative

21

with his love—no hugging or sitting in his lap. Most of all, Daddy was a good Christian man. He made sure we were in church. We saw Mother every other weekend. She was very into her money and getting our love and affection, but she did not show her love to us.

Then it happened. At a very young age, I was sexually abused and threatened with a knife by my half brother.

Growing up without Mother at home was not easy, and the unsettling thoughts about the divorce were buried deep within me. Since school was not a priority, I stayed rather isolated without many friends. The divorce and the abuse by my half brother together made me feel shame, embarrassment, and hurt . . . more than I ever knew. So what did I do? I tucked it all away in my heart until later.

Playing basketball was an outlet for me. My success in the sport brought me out of my shell a bit. I loved being accepted and special because of my athletic talent. I had never been given any encouragement, and Daddy never talked about doing anything after high school. I am the only one of four children who graduated from high school. I even went to college. Without much thought, I married the first guy who came along after high school and had my first child at age eighteen.

Then when I was nineteen, my dad died from cancer. It broke my heart. He had been my rock, my security.

After I received my college degree and became a teacher, my husband left me and our seven-year-old daughter for another woman. I struggled with being abandoned again. Soon after my divorce, I became involved with a married man and stayed in that relationship for thirteen years. It was easier than playing the dating game. It was safe and comfortable. He came and went, and I didn't have to take care of him. He was several years older than me and was more of a father figure to me. He was very controlling, a type that I seemed to attract.

During these thirteen years, I never went to church. There were no singles classes, and a couple's class was definitely not going to happen for me. Their words were, "We don't know what to do with you."

Next I pursued and married a divorced guy I had known for a long time. We were married for ten years when I learned that he had been seeing a younger woman for about a year. Can't believe I didn't see that coming! His leaving was extremely devastating. He was the love of my life. It was the worst pain I had ever felt. I literally went to bed for four months. I was so hurt.

I turned to my church for help but found, at times,

it was only God and me. My pastor walked me through the divorce and showed me about a love relationship with God. He was able to show me that what my husband and I had was not a real marriage.

As a result of my divorce, I started a singles ministry at my church. I love to share and encourage others that God does have a place in His kingdom for singles. "One" can absolutely make a difference in other people's lives.

I remember my pastor telling me after my divorce that God may never send another man into my life—that may not be in His plan. The journey I am on now is to get myself whole again, to really get down to the "nuts and bolts" of God and me, and who He has made me to be. I continue to go to counseling to deal with the issues from the past. God has taken the father role, and I am that piece of clay on the potter's wheel. My joy comes from serving God and helping people.

One of the first Bible studies that I did was *Experiencing God*, from which I learned that you can have a love relationship with God. Studies with authors such as Max Lucado and others, who are Christ-centered, have grounded my faith. The Song of Solomon is a wonderful study of marriage and a revelation of God's plan for marriage in the "big picture" way. He doesn't plan for us to go out to find someone just to have a partner (they are a dime a dozen), but He truly has a plan for your life! I am determined to stay in God's presence, in His house, and with His people.

{ STRANDS of HOPE }

. . . .

Therefore, if anyone is in Christ,
he is a new creation; old things have passed away;
behold, all things have become new.

–2 CORINTHIANS 5:17 NKJV

. . . .

No matter what we've been through, God's love and forgiveness can make all things new. We may still have reminders and consequences. However, we must not dwell on past failures or cripple ourselves with guilt.

Instead, we must take up the life Christ offers and build again. God's forgiveness brings about change and restores us to the person He designed us to be.

Think About It

- Was there ever a time in your life when your innocence was betrayed?

- How has that affected your life?

- Read Luke 23. In verse 34, Jesus asked forgiveness for those who had betrayed Him. Why do you think He did this?

- What might embracing forgiveness look like to you?

Pray About It

Holy and righteous God, You have given me redemption through the blood of Jesus, the forgiveness of sins, according to the riches of Your grace.

Overturn the stones of disobedience that hide my sin and set me free.

Never let me be a victim. Instead let me walk in the victory Christ won for me on the cross.

Open the windows of heaven and flood my mind with memories of Your faithfulness.

Render any areas of darkness in my life to the light of Christ.

Every good and perfect gift comes from You. I am grateful!

Do not let me continue to cycle into unbelief. I want to place all my hope and trust in You.

Amen

Chapter 3

Secrets of the Abused

God created families to be a safe, happy, peaceful place for our children. Unfortunately many parents model rage, manipulate through guilt, and curse their children instead of blessing them. So many times we cause pain for ourselves—and others—when we make choices based solely on our feelings.

We all have probably had this type of pain inflicted on us in one way or another in our lifetimes. Abuse can be physical, verbal, mental, emotional, or sexual. Maybe you can remember a time when you or someone you love felt the sting of abuse.

None of us pass through childhood without some emotional wounds or without believing lies that distort how we see ourselves and how we deal with life.

{ Abuse can be physical, verbal, mental, emotional, or sexual. }

My childhood was so dysfunctional and crazy that I would do anything to get out. And at age seventeen, that's exactly what I did!

I remember the night so well, the night I met the man I thought was going to rescue me. He was ten years my senior, handsome, with gorgeous red hair and a smile that would melt my heart away. I was so flattered that he would even speak to me. We exchanged phone numbers, and I thought I'd never see him again, since he happened to live in another state. Much to my surprise I received a call two weeks later saying that he had moved back to Tennessee. "Wow," I thought, "I must have made a great first impression."

We dated for a whole six months, and I remember the night he asked me to marry him. The night was beautiful with thousands of stars lighting up the sky. As we sat in his car outside my grandmother's house, he asked me the big question. I thought this might be my one and only chance to have someone love, honor, and cherish me, so I said yes.

On September 27, 1974, we were married in the small red-brick church where I had grown up. As my father led me down the aisle, I held my beautiful bouquet of yellow and white daisies, believing we would live happily ever after for the rest of our lives.

Yes, desperate people do desperate things. And I desperately was looking for love.

The first week into my Hallmark Card marriage (you know, where everyone lives happily ever after) I was shocked when he physically took his anger out on me. It was a rage I had never seen before—or maybe I had but just chose to look the other way. My husband's moody cycles and unexpected explosions were painfully familiar to me. It was as though my childhood had followed me right into my marriage.

With each fit of rage, my husband felt remorse and asked for forgiveness, promising it would never happen again. But it did. I thought it might have been my fault because I did not love him the way he needed to be loved, and I told myself I just needed to try harder to please him.

Instead of pulling back the curtains and allowing people to see our unhappy home life, I pretended that everything was okay and kept our secrets in the dark. I always kept a big smile on my face. I did not know that telling the truth could have been so powerful and maybe would have gotten some help in our marriage. Looking back, I now realize I lacked courage and was too proud to tell anyone just because I was worried what people would think.

{ I did not know that telling the truth could have been so powerful. }

During our marriage, I gave birth to two beautiful children, a girl and a boy. The marriage ended after fifteen years. During those fifteen years, there were several affairs that tried to fill that emptiness inside of me. And by this point, my self-worth and self-confidence were nonexistent.

Hearts somehow seem harder to heal than any broken bone! Through God's grace and my ex-husband's continued search for peace, contentment, and happiness, he has now found the calmness in his spirit that has allowed us to remain friends and supportive parents of our children.

Through it all, I know I was the fortunate one. Most abusive relationships never find the resolution that ours has.

Saturday, 9:00 a.m. - Tracy

Tracy is much like most of us. She works nine to five, has a public servant's job, and wears a beautiful smile on her face every day to hide the pain she feels inside. Over the course of many hairdos, she and I found we had a lot in common.

I was asked to write my story. I don't like "my story," and whenever I think about it or talk about it, I usually end up feeling depressed for the next few days. I suppose that this is the reason why I have spent a great deal of time running and trying to forget my own story.

I grew up in an emotionally barren household with an alcoholic mother and an extremely distant father who was bitter about being married and having two children. My mother spent the majority of her time either fighting with my father or trying to keep him from leaving her. My father had one affair (that I know of), and he is still with that person to this day.

When I was eight years old, my father molested me. I justified not telling anyone or holding him accountable because it happened only one time.

Through high school, I had one boyfriend, and at age seventeen, I became pregnant. My boyfriend refused to acknowledge it was his, so my mother took me to Kentucky to have an abortion. I was too far along in my pregnancy to have an abortion in Tennessee.

Between this incident and the fact that I could never please my father, I began hating myself more and more each day. I became rooted in shame. My bad attitude about myself poisoned everything I said and did. I became very promiscuous, while desperately searching for love and acceptance.

I met my first husband when I was eighteen, and I became pregnant at age nineteen. I didn't really love him; I didn't even know what love really was. No one ever taught me, nor did I have very good examples. I was so desperate to leave my house that I married him. We ended up having three children together. He was emotionally abusive and a workaholic. I had numerous affairs during our marriage, which ended in seven years. I am currently married to a man that I do love, but he is an alcoholic—and a very mean one at that. He was recently arrested for DUI and is going to lose his job. Boy, can I pick 'em!

Until recently, I had always "dabbled" in God but never completely gave myself to Him. I do not know what will become of my marriage, but I believe that I am to be still in this season in my life for a reason. With God's love I know I can make it one day at a time. I encourage those of you reading this to meditate on God's Word and apply its principles to your life. It is the only thing that brings me peace in the midst of a storm.

{ STRANDS of HOPE }

Peace I leave with you, My peace I give to you; not as the world gives do I give to you. Let not your heart be troubled, neither let it be afraid.

–JOHN 14:27 NKJV

I don't think anyone ever *chooses* to enter into an abusive relationship. We usually end up there under the illusion that an unfulfilled need will be met by that person. Then, when things turn bad, we often feel—because of fear or circumstances—that it's too late to back out. But we can avoid those relationships by seeking the only One who can fill all of our needs. And if we're already there, in those relationships, we can trust in Him fully to bring us peace.

> He loves turning hopeless situations into amazing possibilities.

No matter what, the problems of this world are only temporary. When we give up control of our lives and place our trust in God, then the peace of God covers our hearts and minds.

God has asked you to trust Him and not to worry: He loves turning hopeless situations into amazing possibilities.

Think About It

- Does peace mean that you will always be free from troubles and conflict? (John 16:33)

- Describe a time when you faced a difficult decision, but you had peace with your decision.

- Can you remember a situation that happened a year, five years, or maybe even ten years ago, and you thought it was the worst thing you have ever been through? Looking back at it, how do you view that situation now?

- Do you realize that worry can steal your peace? Read Philippians 4:6–8.

- Where is the most peaceful place you have ever been? What made it that way?

Pray About It

Precious Lord, teach me to place my trust in You alone. I need Your Holy Spirit to touch my troubled heart, free me from fear, and give me peace.

Enable me to give up control, so that You, O God, can be in full control of every aspect of my life.

Accompany me wherever I go, and give me wisdom to make choices that are pleasing to You.

Cover me with the blood of Jesus, rescue me from the guilt and shame of my past, and give me true freedom in Christ.

Every good and perfect gift comes from You, Lord. I rejoice in the blessings You have given me.

Amen

Chapter 4

Secrets of the Shameful

During my years behind the chair, women have found the courage to discuss a variety of deep and penetrating issues in their lives with me, including abortion. And once again, unfortunately, I could relate.

When an affair is *about* to happen, the parties involved

are usually innocent and blameless—or so they think. A friendship often leads to the sharing of personal information that leads to comforting one another. And the comforting leads to intimacy. The result has *S-I-N* written all over it.

We bring so much pain on ourselves when we make choices based only on our feelings. I never felt "special" or "valued" by my husband. And even though I was in the beauty business,

> {
> We bring so much pain on ourselves when we make choices based only on our feelings.
> }

I didn't feel there was any beauty within me. I just didn't feel that I was "good enough." The years were slipping by without me experiencing the excitement in my marriage. Where was the romance, the internal fireworks, culminating in a trip to the moon?

After six years of marriage, I gave into my lonely, unexcited feelings. I allowed those feelings to drive me into the arms of another man. The consequences of passion are never thought of at that moment. My response to having someone tell me that I was special and beautiful was beyond my expectations. My desperate search for physical love overshadowed my longings to be a wife and mother.

At first, I felt safe and cherished by this man in my life. But all of those warm, fuzzy feelings quickly dissolved when I realized I was pregnant. At the age of twenty-five I was faced with the decision to do what was morally right or to do what (I thought) was the convenient way out. I knew I didn't want everyone to find out, to face public humiliation. Not knowing what to do, I went to—of all people—my husband and told him what had happened. Angry and confused, he and I decided we would stay together and work it out. But neither of us was equipped to handle the constant reminder of my infidelity.

Opting for the convenient solution, I sought help from my medical doctor. He told me that he had a friend who could take care of the situation. Trying to justify my choice, I rationalized that a hospital procedure would not be an abortion. The procedure was called a D&C on my insurance papers. That sounded a lot better than an abortion. Telling myself I had no other choice, I discarded the child that was conceived from an affair.

My husband and I stayed together another nine years after that. We even had another child together. Although he and I never really talked about the incident again, I lived daily with the guilt and pain from the affair and the abortion. Tragically, I still didn't understand what was broken inside of me.

Abortion was taken out of the back alley when it was made legal in 1973. Spiritually speaking, however, abortion remains in the back alley. Many women suffer a spiritual crisis following abortion. I was one of them. And as a result, God has enabled me to nurture and help these women who have confided in me because my circumstances parallel their own. I continually choose to tell my story, praying that women will never again choose abortion.

> { Every child conceived is a child of God. }

Every child conceived is a child of God. The prophet Jeremiah wrote these words from God: "Before I formed you in the womb I knew you" (Jeremiah 1:5). The Bible makes it clear that God sees the tiny embryo as a new life with a future already prepared. How sad it is that many children never live beyond the womb because of abortion.

Women who have had abortions also need the healing touch of the great physician, Jesus Christ. An angry crowd once brought to Jesus a woman who had been caught in sin. She was morally guilty. Yet, Jesus focused on her restoration. As the Son of God, He was able to forgive her sin and give her healing and wholeness (John 8:11). God's love and mercy are all-encompassing. There's nothing that you can do that is beyond the bounds of His grace.

Saturday, 12:00 p.m. – Beth

Beth, like me, has a story to tell about making choices that she would later regret. She also learned about forgiveness and the depth of God's love and grace in her life.

Let me begin by telling you a little about my mother and the events surrounding my early childhood. My mother was married with two small children when her husband was killed in a car accident. Mother had experienced some problems with depression prior to the accident, and the trauma of the accident caused her almost to "lose it" completely.

In the period following the accident, she became pregnant out of wedlock. She chose to terminate this pregnancy with an abortion. Following a similar pattern, she soon became pregnant again. This pregnancy resulted in the birth of a baby girl that my mother gave up for adoption. The pattern of behavior continued with two more pregnancies that resulted in my birth and the birth of my baby sister. The result of the downward spiral my mother experienced in her life was four out of wedlock pregnancies that added two children to the two she and her husband had before the accident.

As you can imagine, my mother had a very difficult time raising four children alone. When I was two years old, she met another man and chose to leave her children to be with him. My older brother and sister went to live with their father's parents. I went to live with my maternal grandparents. My baby sister was adopted by my aunt and uncle. I don't remember much about this period in my childhood other than a nagging sense of sadness and a constant fear of being abandoned that I carried into my adult life. During my childhood my mother would visit on occasion. She did not always come when she promised, but she always left me again. As I look back on my childhood, it probably would have been better if she had stayed away.

As I grew older, I began to resent my mother. I felt that something was missing in my life because I did not have a mother or father in my life. My grandparents were sixty-six and seventy-two. They loved me and provided for all of my needs. However, they were not very affectionate and did not talk to me very much. My grandfather died when I was twelve, leaving another void in my life. All through these early years and into my teen years, I was searching for the love and affection that was missing in my life.

When I was seventeen, I became pregnant the first time I was with a boy. I was so scared of what my grandmother would think. I knew I would be such a disappointment to her. She was always telling me how I was just like my mother, and she did not mean it in a positive way. She had always reminded me of the burden on her because of my mother's mistakes. I also worried about what my friends would think of me. I had always made good grades and was very involved in school. I didn't want this to ruin my reputation. My grandmother was constantly telling me that "a good name is worth more than silver and gold." I was now questioning my self-worth and how I could possibly be a good mother while struggling with depression and feelings of low self-esteem. I was to start college in the fall, and a baby just did not fit into the picture.

As you probably have noticed, everything was all about me. I never really thought of the baby inside of me as a human being. Having never been around babies or pregnant women, it just didn't seem possible that there was a living human being inside me. I had no idea that at ten weeks, when I discovered I was pregnant, the baby's heart was already beating; it had fully formed fingers and toes and could even hiccup.

Regardless, I made the decision to have the abortion. The procedure itself was physically painful. I can remember having a sense of relief that it was all over, but no real feeling of guilt at that time. I simply tried to block it all out of my mind. Later I did occasionally wonder if I would be able to have children or if God would allow me to become pregnant again.

Ten years later I was pregnant with a baby for which I had planned very carefully. I had intentionally waited to have a baby until I could be a stay-at-home mom. Since my mother had not been there for me, I was determined that I was going to be there for my kids.

On my first visit to the doctor, I heard my baby's heart beating and saw him on the ultrasound. It looked like he waved to me, and I felt him kicking. At that point, I realized what I had done to my first child. Great sadness came over me, even though I was so happy to be having this child. I feared that something terrible would happen to him because of the abortion.

Fortunately, God put a friend in my life who was a strong Christian. She was four years younger than I, but very mature in her faith. I had grown up believing that I had to earn my salvation. Even though I had been baptized when I was eight years old, I knew I had done something horrible that could keep me from going to heaven. I then experienced two dreams that made me fully understand that I was not saved.

My friend showed me two verses in the Bible that helped me understand salvation. Ephesians 2:8–9 says, "For by grace you have been saved through faith, and that not of yourselves; it is the gift of God, not of works, lest anyone should boast" (NKJV). When I realized that my salvation was not based on what I did, but on what Jesus did on my behalf on the cross, I asked for forgiveness and was saved.

Three years later I had another baby, a girl. The joy of a new baby again brought the remorse and reality of what I had done. I had asked God for forgiveness countless times. I know now that He forgave me the first time I asked. I was just unable to forgive myself.

My first marriage ended in divorce, but I was blessed

to have a second chance with a wonderful Christian man for whom I thank God every day. I was also blessed with two stepdaughters and another precious son.

Although I still had times when I felt guilty about the abortion. I thought that if I could just do something to help fight abortion, maybe I would feel better. I kept driving by the Pregnancy Counseling Center thinking I should volunteer. One day I called and spoke with the director. She told me that I would need to complete a training program before I could volunteer, which I did. Because of my abortion, I completed a post-abortion Bible study. It was a wonderful study that has helped me deal with many issues in my life.

I just want any woman who has had an abortion to know that there is forgiveness through the blood of Jesus no matter what circumstances surrounded your abortion. There is no sin so bad that God won't forgive—if you just ask.

And for any woman who is facing an unplanned pregnancy, there is hope for you too. There is the consideration of adoption. Many couples are unable to have children of their own. You can be an incredible blessing for them through adoption.

I want to encourage everyone to get involved in some way in the fight against abortion. Over a century ago our country realized the evils of slavery. We look back now and wonder how anyone could ever have thought it was appropriate to keep another person in bondage. Why then does our country think it is appropriate to kill millions of innocent babies? Although many people know that abortion is wrong, we still do not do enough to address the problem.

Wednesday, 3:00 p.m. – Katie

Many of you can relate to Katie. She is a hard working single mom who is totally dedicated to her children. Her beautiful smile is one of the first things you notice about her. Since becoming a Christian, her life has never been the same.

I grew up in San Diego, California, in a dysfunctional family. My father, who was in the navy, was an alcoholic. I don't remember much about my father, except the games we played when he was at home. At the time the games were fun games that seemed to make Daddy happy. Later I realized what my father had done to me.

I was four years old when my mother and father divorced. My brother was seventeen, my older sister was seven, and my little sister was three at the time. Daddy did not visit us, and Mom was always gone, leaving us on our own. My mother brought home many different men over the years. They did not stay very long. Many of the men did what they wanted to us and left. The abuse was rampant in our home. After my dad, there was also sexual abuse from my mom's boyfriends.

We were neglected because Mom worked long hours to support us. We were physically abused by my older sister in the name of discipline. The combination of the abuse created an environment in our home that was emotionally devastating to the children involved.

At the age of twelve, I attended my first drinking party and never stopped after that. I would party all night and then go to school the next morning. I reached out to Jesus through an after-school Bible study. I knew I needed help, but I was not sure where to find help. The following year the Bible study was removed from the school. That ended any Christian-based training for me. (One has to wonder how many people would benefit from prayer in school.)

My first boyfriend was John. I was twelve and impressed to have the attention. He was a wonderful boy and really cared about me. We were best friends until my party life took charge. I began to do exactly what I wanted to do without thinking about the impact my actions would have on my life or the lives of the people around me.

In the eighth grade my life went from bad to worse. I knew I wanted to be loved, but I didn't know how to find it. I was alone. I started searching for love in older navy men I met while babysitting for the neighbors. I had never had sex with my boyfriend, John. I finally convinced him that having sex was the only way for him to prove his love for me. After we became intimate, we would get drunk and have sex every time we were together.

During the next three years, I broke up and reconciled with John several times. One night he caught me with another guy. I learned quickly that the best way to get rid of a guy was to cheat on him. Whenever I got tired of a relationship, I would move on to the next one.

At the age of nineteen, I started college. Instead of receiving an education, I became pregnant. I felt I had no one to turn to. No one would tell me what to do in spite of the options before me. The decision was mine. The father of the child did not want children, and I did not want to be alone. He said he loved me, yet I was alone. He said he would be there, but I went to the clinic and signed the papers for the abortion alone. He was only the driver. He never talked to me about what I had done.

One year later we were still together. I was again facing the same situation of being alone and pregnant. I made the decision to keep the baby no matter what. I knew that I would lose him. I made my first doctor's appointment. I heard the baby's heartbeat after only eight weeks. I told the father about the doctor's visit and the heartbeat. His reaction was to tell me that it was not fair for me to have his child when we were not ready. I tried to discuss the issues surrounding the pregnancy, but he reacted in anger.

When I was fourteen weeks pregnant, he convinced me to check into the procedure, and I was shocked to learn that an abortion could still be done at this point in the pregnancy. However, the decision had to be made immediately. Feeling alone again, I believed that I could not ask God for help because He was not with me. I thought that I would have no more worries. Everything would be fine after the procedure!

This is my story about the two children I conceived that never had a chance. I wasn't ready to be a single mother, and the father wanted nothing to do with a child. I talked about adoption, but he could not stand the thought. I did not want to kill my babies. I knew it was wrong. But I knew if I wanted him to stay with me, I could not bring home a baby. Still, even without a baby, he didn't stay with me.

I am now a single mom raising three girls, just like my mom. The difference is that I have a God who loves me, a wonderful church family, and the one thing I have longed for my whole life: I have the love of my heavenly Father. He will always love and protect me. His grace is sufficient for me . . . and for you.

Please know that you are not alone. I can look back now and see that God was just waiting for me to cry out to Him.

[STRANDS of HOPE]

Praise be to the God and Father of our Lord Jesus Christ, the Father of compassion and the God of all comfort, who comforts us in all our troubles, so that we can comfort those in any trouble with the comfort we ourselves have received from God.

–2 CORINTHIANS 1:3–4

Despite the horrible guilt that comes after an abortion, we three women have all survived and found the loving forgiveness and grace of God. Our wonderful God is the source of every mercy and the One who so graciously comforts and strengthens us in our hardships and trials—even our ungodly decisions. Why does He do this? So that when others are troubled, needing our sympathy and encouragement, we can pass on to them this same help and comfort God has given us.

We may still have reminders and consequences. But we have learned, through grace, that we must not dwell on past failures or cripple ourselves with guilt. Instead, we must take up the life Christ offers and build again. God's forgiveness brings about change and restores us to the person He designed us to be.

Think About It

- What kinds of things in your past do you find hardest to let go?

- Read Psalm 23:3. What is a restored soul? What seems to accompany a restored soul?

- Have you forgiven yourself for past mistakes? Why or why not? How might that change your future?

- What do you believe God wanted you to learn from these experiences?

Pray About It

Gracious and loving God, thank You for Your redeeming grace.

Redeem me by the blood of Christ, forgive my sins, and help me to forgive myself.

Accept my life as a humble offering, and use my hands to bless others.

Create a sanctuary of peace and joy in my heart by continually filling me with Your Spirit.

Equip me with everything I need to do Your perfect will.

Amen

Chapter 5

Secrets of the Lonely Heart

The beauty pageant was in full swing. As the junior high girls pranced across the stage in their exquisite gowns and their-one-of-a-kind hairdos, the cheers from friends and family filled the auditorium. The hairdressers in our town had once again thrilled the judges with their exceptional talent, and the pageant would raise thousands of dollars for local charities.

I was standing in the hallway of the school waiting for my girls to come out of the dressing room, when there before me stood a tall, handsome, smooth-talking man who put his hand on my shoulder and whispered words that would change the direction of my life for many years. At this point, I was still in a marriage with a husband with whom I could not communicate my needs, hurts, and longings. And something deep inside of me knew that I was looking for that special someone who would say all the right things I needed to hear and bring me the romance and fireworks I sought.

Little did I know that the man who had flattered me that night at the pageant by telling me, "You deserve so much more," would be the same man who would bring that excitement into my life. He was also married, but he let me know I deserved an exciting, fun, handsome man like himself. After a while, we left our spouses behind and quickly married. I sure got the fireworks I had been searching for—explosions and all!

I sure got the fireworks I had been searching for—explosions and all!

Not long into the marriage, my illusions of this perfect love ended. The laughter turned into sobs, and late-night drinking binges ended up being ten times more emotionally and physically abusive than anything I had experienced with my first husband. I wasn't the only one who suffered for my bad choices. My son and daughter also had to bear his insults, along with the trauma of hearing the man beat their mother. Parents, *mothers,* are supposed to protect their children. Yet there were many times I failed to put my children first for fear of him leaving me. What was I thinking?

Professionally, I had plenty of courage and business savvy, but when it came to personal relationships with men, I was poor, weak, and needy. I thought it was better to have someone, even if he was abusive, than to be alone. For me, the silence of loneliness yelled, "Nobody loves you! Nobody ever wanted you!" Loneliness can be a killer of the heart and soul.

> When it came to personal relationships with men, I was poor, weak, and needy.

I felt like I was going to die as I suffered through the many nights he never came home. Sadness engulfed my heart. What was he doing? Who was he with? When will he be home? How will he act when he does get home? Fear of the unknown haunted me. Our home life was like walking on eggshells. I had to be careful not to say or do anything wrong, because it could result in days of silence.

I sought help for our marriage and his alcohol addiction

through several recovery programs. However, for recovery programs to work, both parties must want the same results. Needless to say, ours didn't work. After six years of marriage, my husband decided that he did not love me anymore and walked away from me and my children.

Still, it is always the darkest before the dawn. No man, no fireworks, no love. I wish I had realized that God was there with me in the pit, loving me warts and all.

Tuesday, 10:00 a.m. – Anna

Anna always looks like an undercover cop. Dark sunglasses and a baseball hat is a sure sign of a bad hair day. Nevertheless, Anna is a beautiful redhead, tall in stature with a heart as big as Texas. She works as a nurse and is a devoted wife, mother, and friend. She truly loves the Lord with all her heart.

My earliest memories are not of a loving home with lots of hugs and kisses. Mother was surely around, but I remember little of her. I felt lost in the shuffle of a house full of children. I do, however, recall an alcoholic father who was gruff and stern when sober, and down-right mean when drunk. The sight of his truck driving down the road, weaving and jerking erratically, caused me to run for my baby bottle and dive under the bed to hide until he left again or went to bed. "I love you" did not seem to apply to any of the children in my family.

I grew up feeling unloved and of no value. My first marriage occurred just twenty days before my twentieth birthday. Two years later we had a beautiful baby girl. When she was one year old, her daddy, my husband, was killed in an automobile accident.

As a twenty-five-year-old widow with a child, I accepted the marriage proposal of another man. Two years into this marriage, we had a beautiful son with curly red hair. One day I was watching him in his crib, and he seemed to be grasping for air. I screamed for my husband to call for help as I tried to give the baby CPR. My husband panicked and ran out of the house, but I was able to dial the phone for help. However, it was too late. The baby stopped breathing before the doctor could drive the five miles to our house.

After our son's death, my husband became very abusive to my daughter. Although we had another child together, he resented my daughter being alive instead of our son. Our home life worsened, and we decided to divorce. I stepped out in faith and moved my children away so I could attend college for a nursing degree.

During my second semester of school, I became ill with Hepatitis A and was in bed for two months. My daughter spent much of this time with her paternal grandparents, and my son was with his father for weeks at a time. I began to spend time with my divorced sister going to bars. I enjoyed the attention I got there. Looking for love in the wrong place, I met my next husband, a womanizer and alcoholic, in a bar.

We settled into married life and I began to attend a charismatic church regularly, which gave me a new sense of peace. My husband would complain that I read the Bible all the time, but he would also comment that he wished for the same peace that I seemed to have. He continued the drinking and partying, coming home at all hours and often after I had left for work. Then he began to work away from home, only showing up on the weekends. After seven years of marriage, I became a divorced woman again.

While working at a hospital, I began to socialize with friends I'd met there. When I was not on call, I'd go dancing with them and, for the first time in my forty years of life, began to drink alcohol. Once again I was drawn to an unhealthy relationship when I met a good-looking man who came on to me, showing me attention that I never felt I deserved. After dating a couple of months, he wanted to move in with me. Because of my children, I refused to live with him until we were married. He was happy to oblige. It should have been a major red flag that he had been married and divorced five times, but I was happy that someone wanted me. It didn't take long to see the problems. I think he had eight or nine jobs in the four years we were married. We were soon divorced, and I was a three-time loser!

I began dancing and partying again to cover my loneliness. The laughing face I put on for others was a mask for the pain I was feeling inside. I had given up on God, but He continued to pull at my heart. Deep down, I knew He had not given up on me.

I met an old rodeo buddy of my brother's who was a wonderful, kind, and caring man. We had dated for almost a year when he collapsed one night just after we'd returned from a bull-riding event. He was in cardiac shock and learned at the hospital that he would require a heart transplant. He was an only child with no children and no family to care for him. He needed me, and I needed someone to take care of. On July 30, 1989, we were married. He received his heart transplant the following March. His complete recovery was not to be, and after we were married two short years, he died from complications.

I was so lost and lonely. I was fooled into thinking that perhaps I could be happy again with yet another man. Thirteen months after my husband had died, I found him. My new husband knew I was left in good financial shape. But when the money ran out, so did he!

In the mess of my life, I finally realized that I needed God. I fell down on my face crying out to God, asking Him to forgive me and save me from the life I was living. God heard my cry. He had been there all that time waiting for my return, just like the prodigal son.

After my experience with God, my friend called to say her brother would like to meet me. A month later he e-mailed, saying he didn't want to spend the remainder of his life alone, and asked if we could begin e-mailing each other. Even though we were different, we had a long-distance relationship for about eighteen months until I was able to take early retirement from my job. I sold my home and moved to the state where he had lived. I married for the seventh and FINAL time. My husband is a truly wonderful Christian man who lives what he believes. We are very financially secure with a beautiful home, everything we need, and more.

I truly looked for love in all of the wrong places. I pray that other women will come to know that God through Jesus Christ is the ONLY ONE who will NEVER, EVER let you down.

Friday, 10:00 a.m. – Laura

I just love Laura. Let me tell you, this woman has an addiction to hairspray. She always has to have the last squirt. I've done Laura's hair for thirty years. From my perch behind the chair, I can remember so many things that Laura has confided to me. I vividly remember the day she sat in my chair and made the comment, "I will never have to worry about my husband cheating on me." Laura remembers it too.

I can so well remember making that statement. In my mind I didn't think I would ever have to confront the circumstances surrounding unfaithfulness in my marriage. I look back now at the events of the year that the affair happened and realize what a very hard year it was. Even given all of the factors that were taking place that year, I never dreamed it could happen to us.

For the first time in our lives we were going in

65

separate directions. I was taking care of a little girl we had adopted who had some developmental problems. My life was full with the adopted child and our two other children. Our son was busy trying to secure scholarships for college. Our daughter was in the eighth grade preparing for high school. In the middle of the normal chaos in our lives, my mother's house burned. She moved in with us for four months while her new house was being built.

While I didn't recognize all of the symptoms at the time, I noticed my husband doing strange things. He would just sit in the house like he was depressed or in a fog. He became distant and cold toward me. He appeared to never have time for any of the children. I discussed my husband's behavior with our pastor. He seemed to think David was going through a midlife crisis. After all, he was about to hit the big 4-0! Still, an affair never crossed my mind.

David continued to lead the singing at church. He taught a Bible class and sometimes filled in for our preacher. Little did I know that he was leading a double life. David was my soul mate. I couldn't imagine either of us being with anyone else.

On the Sunday night before Thanksgiving 2001, my world fell apart. I pulled into the parking lot of our business to find him sitting in the car with another woman. That is when I knew. My world just fell out from under me. As I was pulling out to leave, he was walking over to me saying, "It is not what you think." I went berserk. All of the pieces began to fall into place.

I immediately sought the counsel of my pastor. I did not want to see or talk to my husband. My pastor encouraged me to go home and find out more about the situation. David maintained his story that nothing had happened. The two had met that evening to call things off because an affair could hurt many people. I so much wanted to believe him. Our pastor and his wife cautioned me to be careful until I was sure that I knew the whole story.

In the days that followed, I kept close tabs on David. I no longer trusted him to do what he said or be where he said he was going. He was aware of my early warning in our marriage: "If you are ever with another woman, I will leave you! I will not stay!"

The next event that occurred involved the husband of the woman David was seeing. When he learned of the affair, he wanted to meet with us. David continued to deny that any physical contact had occurred. The meeting proved to be a revealing session for all involved. David was thrown under the bus by the woman when she revealed all of the gross details, including dates and places.

I was then faced with the decision of my early threat. Do I leave him or do I stay and try to work it out? I told David he could stay in the house until we made a decision as to what we were going to do. I made no promises.

David immediately tried to make everything right. He made a statement in church in front of everybody about his life, how he had lied and hurt his family. He stepped down as a deacon, which defaced him publicly. He tried in the next several months to regain the ground he had lost with his children and me. He planned a renewal of our vows. He wrote the invitations and a poem for the service because he wanted everyone to know that he wanted his family and his wife back. I was hesitant and nervous about the whole situation. Our pastor reminded me that this does not mean that everything goes away. It is only a renewing, a stepping stone. This is the first step on a path to reconciliation.

David and I began marriage counseling. Many people think that counseling is a quick fix. Believe me, it is not. We had three appointments a week for over a year. I believe you can NEVER let your guard down.

Satan is alive and well. He is not happy that the situation turned out the way it did. Satan walks around every day seeking to destroy and devour. He devoured us once and he knows our weak points. Even with counseling, we still have our weak points. But I believe that the Lord does not want us to lead a defeated life. He longs for us to have a life full of joy, even through crisis situations.

{ STRANDS of HOPE }

. . . .

Love the LORD your God with all your heart and with all your soul and with all your strength.

—DEUTERONOMY 6:5

. . . .

The intimacy offered by our sometimes shallow, shabby society is typically in terms of one-night stands, candlelit evenings, or a smoke-filled nightclub. Our hearts, minds, and desires are lured to these counterfeit offers of intimacy, but they are not what our soul craves. Every time we dip into these mirages, we come up empty.

We are built for intimacy with God, and it cannot be purchased at the corner newsstand. The intimacy we long for is found in a growing relationship with the One who is perfectly suited to satisfy and sustain us. We can enjoy *true* intimacy as we grow more deeply conscious of, connected to, and confident in God and Him alone, our unfailing resource in life.

Think About It

- Has your heart been longing and loving somewhere else?

- Do you love God with all that you are and have? If not, what baggage must you get rid of to renew that relationship?

- What one thing can you do today to demonstrate your love for God?

- Read John 4:1–26 about Jesus and the Samaritan woman at the well. How has Jesus put together the broken pieces from your life?

Pray About It

Redeemer, Father, Lover of my Soul, help me to truly love You with all my heart.

Enable me to clearly see sin, repent, and turn from darkness to light.

Set my feet firmly on The Rock of Jesus Christ, so that my foundation will not be shaken.

Teach me to hide Your Word in my heart, so that I will not sin against You.

Overflow my cup with godly love.

Restore all that the enemy has stolen from me.

Establish a fortress of love and mercy within me.

Do immeasurably more in my life than I can ask or imagine.

Amen

Chapter 6

Secrets of the Hurting

"That which doesn't kill us will only make us stronger." I remember reading those words of wisdom somewhere, but when your heart has been totally ripped out of your chest, words of inspiration are of little comfort.

I had not seen or heard from my husband for a couple of days. This erratic behavior had been going on for quite some time. It was early Monday morning; the children had already gone to school when I heard the sounds of a car squealing up the driveway. I pulled back the drapes in the bedroom, and much to my surprise, there sat a silver sports car with the trunk up. I felt my heart sink; I knew why he was here.

Very few words were spoken as he threw his clothes, shoes, and six years of marriage into the back of the car for the last time. His clothes had been in and out of the house so many times, they were worn threadbare, but something told me it wouldn't happen again. I began to cry and beg, hoping that maybe this last ditch effort would manipulate him into staying and keeping my false hopes alive. I had worked so hard trying to keep up the appearances of a happy family, when the entire world knew differently. I was only fooling myself.

{ I was angry because I was powerless over what was happening in my life. }

I found it difficult to be comforted by God, or anyone else for that matter. I was wounded and broken! I was angry because I was powerless over what was happening in my life. I knew God could do something, but He didn't. I laid on my bed that night, crying and screaming, "Well, God, here I am! Alone again! Do You even care?"

Saturday, 12:00 p.m. – Donna

On the outside, Donna is sugar and spice and everything nice. But the smile she wears doesn't always hide the hurt that she feels inside.

I am a true New Yorker! My parents divorced when I was sixteen years old. As the youngest child, I decided to live with my dad and quickly became his caretaker. I never even considered college because I was so scared that I couldn't learn with my disability of dyslexia. Everything I did presented a challenge when it came to academics.

By the age of nineteen, I was married to Jim and working as a cashier at a local grocery store. I worked so hard that I progressed quickly to a management position. I loved the energy I got from helping people.

After the first year of marriage, Jim and I started having some marital problems. You know when you're young, you sometimes think, "The grass is greener on the other side of the fence"—only to find out it's just another field. Deciding a change in scenery would help, we moved to Atlanta. I had never been anywhere outside New York. Talk about culture shock!

Knowing we wanted our marriage to work, Jim and I thought a child would be just what we needed. After efforts through fertility medicine and artificial insemination failed, we surprisingly got pregnant on our own.

We had our first child, a boy, on July 7, 2003, and we named him Luke. Jim was on the fast track in his company and was soon promoted to a new position in Nashville, Tennessee. He worked seventeen-hour-a-day shifts, which hindered him in bonding with Luke because he was always gone. We had no friends, and we were not attending church anywhere. We just existed.

The stress of Jim's job began to cause him terrible migraines, and he resigned his job. He left a fabulous salary, but he couldn't take the stress any longer. The best part of that decision was that he could now bond with his son. We didn't have a lot of money, so we had to be creative. We went on walks, went to the zoo, and sometimes just sat in our home and played with Luke.

We truly became a family, something I had longed to have.

After three months of family bonding, Jim started a new job. Then one day something happened that changed our entire lives. Jim was out of town, and Luke developed a fever. Even with the medicine prescribed by our pediatrician, Luke did not improve. I put him to bed, and the next morning he was lethargic. The doctor of the local clinic said he must have a virus. Luke continued to get worse. Our precious son was very sick. Fear gripped us as we were sent to Vanderbilt's Children's Hospital where he was placed in critical care. I made a call to my mother, and said, "Mom, I'm scared!" Jesus was preparing us and beginning to teach us what a family really was.

They put Luke on a respirator, and he tried so hard to fight. Luke was diagnosed with XLA disease, an inherited immune deficiency disease, which results in the body's inability to produce antibodies. Soon after, Luke died there in my arms.

Even though I only had my son for a short time, Luke taught me about Jesus:

• about unconditional love and compassion,

- about the simple things, and

- that it's not what you have; it's what you give.

Assured that Luke was in heaven, I wanted to know how to get to him. Thankfully, my aunt encouraged Jim and me to go back to church, and amazingly the church body wrapped its arms around us and showed us God's love.

There still are times when I feel in deep despair, but there are a few things I manage to do that give me strength, comfort, and direction.

- Put on praise music.

- Read Scripture.

- Journal on happy or sad days.

- Always be in contact with someone who will listen.

- Do not be afraid to ask for help.

I can truly say, with God's help, I have learned to have contentment and peace in my life. But I wait with anticipation to meet Jesus one day and see my son standing with open arms to greet me in heaven.

These are the words that my heart whispers to him:

I thought of you today,
but that is nothing new;
I thought of you yesterday
And days before that too.
I think of you in silence,
I often speak your name,
But all I have are memories
And your picture in a frame.
Your memory is my keepsake
With which I'll never part;
God has you in His keeping;
I have you in my heart.

Thursday, 9:00 a.m. – Patty

Hidden behind those dark designer glasses and a jolly personality is an amazing woman who has experienced the dreadful dark valleys that life sometimes brings.

When I was eleven, my parents divorced, a result of affairs by both my mother and father. I believe the hardest thing I experienced as a child was being asked by the judge who I wanted to live with. (Please never do this to a child!) I was eleven years old and being pulled like a rubber band. The court gave custody to my father, because they said my mother had deserted us.

She had to go back to court several times before she got us back. I never heard my father say, "I love you," but Mother always showed us lots of love. Mother was killed in an automobile accident, and Dad, now an angry old man, is in the nursing home.

I was so desperate to leave home that I researched the idea to go into the military. Then at age eighteen, I met the love of my life. We ran off, got married, and kept it a secret for six weeks. We have been married for thirty-four years now, and in our vows I told him I would never divorce him and put our children through what I went through as a child.

Three years after we married, we had our first child. A year later, the same date and just ten minutes apart, we had our second child. I have so many memories of our children growing up. Life was good, until we experienced the most painful tragedy of our lives.

We had all gone on a fabulous cruise to the Bahamas. Shortly after we got back, our sixteen-year-old son started to get sick. He had been experiencing a lot of pain and weight loss, and his color was beginning to change. He just wasn't able to function very well.

He had to be homeschooled. We took him to a doctor in Nashville, and they told us his white count was extremely high. Then we heard the words no mother or father ever wants to hear, "I'm sorry, but your son has leukemia."

They admitted him immediately into the hospital. He received blood, chemo, and radiation, which made him amazingly better. The doctors gave us a very positive prognosis.

Life doesn't always play fairly, and my little boy died ten months after he was diagnosed. When my son died, I lost my future. All the things parents get to experience, like graduations, weddings, and grandchildren, my husband and I will never have.

Psalm 23 was read every night at midnight when my son was in the hospital. It was God's Word that comforted us during this time.

Joy for me today is enjoying family and being in God's service. My husband and I became foster parents after our son's death. I love children so much, and we wanted to share our blessings with them. My sister just buried her son at age seventeen, and I wanted to reach out to her, so I wrote her this letter to let know she was not alone.

Hi Sis,

I don't really know how to start, other than to say there is nothing anyone can say or do to make this better. I do know that with the help of God and time the pain does ease. It will never go away!

I am sure that if you haven't laid or slept on his bed, you will. If you haven't gone to his closet and smelled his clothes, you will. For months when the door opens or a car pulls up, you will think it must be your son coming home, because sometimes you forget.

People will ask how you're doing. They want to say something but do not know what else to say. I am sure you will tell them, "Fine," knowing the whole time your heart feels as though it's been ripped from your chest.

Things will return to their regular routine, and people will not come over as much. If you ever want to talk about Greg and the good times, we will talk all day and cry into the night. We were both blessed to have had such wonderful sons; they both left such beautiful legacies. I believe, just like you, Greg was chosen to help others. He will be missed by all of us.

I feel confident when Greg went to those pearly gates,

my son was there to welcome him in. I'm sure they are singing beautiful songs of praise to our Lord.

I love you, Sis!

{ STRANDS of HOPE }

. . . .

To everything there is a season,
A time for every purpose under heaven.

—ECCLESIASTES 3:1 NKJV

. . . .

In beautiful poetry, Solomon reminds us that life continues to march on through a series of uncontrollable situations. There will be times for birth, death, weeping, mourning, laughing, silence, war, and even peace. As joyous or painful as they may be, these are all natural parts of life. When a change is painful, we can trust that God has a purpose in it. When we have God in our lives, we can trust Him through the changes, knowing that every day that passes brings us a little closer to our eternal destiny, to be in the presence of God Himself.

Think About It

- What seasons of life have caused you to be the happiest or the saddest?

- Life challenges can help us grow. What things have you learned through these seasons of your life?

- Do you truly rest in the fact that when life fails you, God will be there to catch you?

- No one is immune to suffering and pain. Describe how you think Jesus might have felt the day He died for you.

- Read the book of Job. At the height of a wonderful life, Job lost everything, including his children and his health. In hard times we don't always need answers as much as we need God and the presence of good faithful friends.

Pray About It

Holy omnipotent God, You see my innermost parts and love me anyway. I am grateful for Your unfailing love.

Everything that happens to me in this life is a signpost pointing me straight into Your arms.

Apart from You, I can do nothing, but with Christ all things are possible.

Lead me in paths of righteousness, forgive my sins, and give me the power of the Holy Spirit to walk in victory.

Enable me to find wholeness in Christ, living the abundant life that Jesus paid for on the cross.

Deliver me from despair and clothe me in a garment of praise, so that I can be joyful no matter what my circumstances may be.

Amen

Chapter 7

Secrets of the Lost

As a child, we never had to guess what we would be doing on Sunday morning. Believe it or not, I went to church all my life. We lived just down the road, so we were there every time the doors were open. I had heard about this Jesus, even had my name on the church roll, but I had no relationship with Him except when I was in a crisis and needed a rescue.

As an adult, I fought to keep up my Christian appearance. I did all of the things good Christian women do . . . and a lot of the things that they *did not*. Sometimes you work so hard to keep up appearances on the outside, it's impossible to let anyone know what's really hurting on the inside. I was running from relationship to relationship, looking for what was missing from within. I was miserable, and I knew I had to make some changes.

Fortunately, there are no appearances to keep up with God. He knows everything about us. Psalm 139 declares:

> O LORD, you have searched me
> and you know me.
> You know when I sit and when I rise;
> you perceive my thoughts from afar.
> You discern my going out and my lying down;
> you are familiar with all my ways.
> Before a word is on my tongue
> you know it completely, O LORD.

> —vv. 1–4

During the morning service at First Baptist Church on September 14, 1997, the God who knew everything about me called my name. I came down the aisle and the pastor lead me in a prayer that changed my life forever. Guess where I was when God called? I was in the choir, of course! I looked like a Christian, talked like one, and even sang like one. But it was all head knowledge, not heart knowledge. I never imagined that I could really be forgiven from the past that haunted me. But 2 Corinthians promises that I could be made new, and this time I was clinging to that

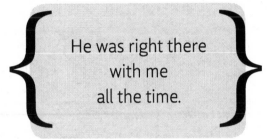

He was right there with me all the time.

promise. (To learn more about making this decision yourself, see Looking for Answers? on p.149.)

The most amazing part is that it was a free gift. I didn't have to perform or be perfect to receive it. I had gone from desperately searching for love to knowing who *is* love—and discovering that He was right there with me all the time.

Saturday, 12:30 p.m. - Diana

Diana's reflection of beauty comes not only from her dark auburn hair but also from within the walls of her quiet—but not shy—soul. Two words come to mind when I think of her: *compassionate* and *encouraging*. A registered nurse by trade, she encourages all those around her to entrust their to-do list to God. She tells me, "He knows better than you what really needs to be accomplished today!"

My mother was very strict, to put it mildly. I now recognize that she was probably a manic depressive. We existed best by constantly pleasing her or just being invisible. My stepfather sexually abused me from the age of five for several years. I certainly didn't want to risk telling this to my mother, so I grew up with many secrets.

I desperately wanted to be normal and accepted by my friends. I joined all of the "right" activities, made the right grades, and was friends with the right people. I had all the right clothes and accessories—even attended charm school—but I always felt like I didn't belong. God gave me many talents, and I used them as a child to occupy myself and as a teen to gain acceptance.

As an adult, I continued to use these talents and began developing some confidence in who I was. I took pride that I was able to put my childhood behind me and become who I chose to be—which was really just whatever others needed me to be. I even began to forget what was inside of me. But God remembered—and He wanted more for me.

When God is doing a work in you, it is sometimes painful. As an adult I had developed a good relationship with my mother. Those habits of always trying to please her remained, and I always felt like a little girl around her. All of that changed nine years ago. I have always been very protective of my daughters, so one day I decided to share about my sexual abuse with them. In her innocence, one of the girls told my mother, and she confronted me. Suddenly the mother of my childhood was back, and she chose to believe I had lied about the sexual abuse.

My mother wrote me long letters of how the wrath of God would strike me down for lying. I eventually had to stop having any contact with her. I spent many nights on the porch crying out to God, asking Him why. The more I prayed, the more abandoned I felt. I can't tell you how many tears I shed. I would get the occasional birthday or Christmas card with the same sentiment: "You are going to burn in hell." It got humorous after a while. The outside of the card would say, "Jesus is the Reason," and inside: "You will burn. Love, Mother."

Eventually, I quit asking God why and began to close my heart to Him. I thought God had abandoned me too, so I turned from my faith. But thank God, He didn't give up on me; He just continued to work. One day I heard a song that said, "There's nothing left of me but what I pretend to be." And I knew I couldn't pretend anymore. I was miserable without Him. I did not know who I was in Him, but I knew who I was out of Him: an orphan needing a loving parent.

Stripped completely bare, I began to be clothed in God's word. He began giving me scripture after scripture. Psalm 27:10: "When my father and my mother forsake me, then the LORD will take care of me" (NKJV). Jeremiah 31:3: "I have loved you with an everlasting love. Therefore with loving kindness I have drawn you" (NKJV).

How humbling it is to know that He sought me out to show His love for me. Peace and love have taken the place of hurt and abandonment in my life. I know He is faithful to complete any work He sets His hands to, and I have seen that evidence clearly in my life. This past year has been a year of miracles and restoration. For the first time in ten years, my mother and I spent Christmas together. I've learned that when I trust Him with the details of my life, things work out much better than I could have ever planned.

Friday, 4:00 p.m. – Linda

I discovered very quickly that Linda is a brilliant mind wrapped up in a beautiful woman. She is small in stature, but has a will that can move mountains.

I am a Jew, and I am now a Jew who now knows her Lord and Savior Jesus Christ.

I did as our original ancestors did and wandered lost in the desert for some forty-odd years before I figured it all out. I am now closing in on half a century on this earth, and there is not a day that I ever allow to pass without thanking our precious God for bringing me to Him. I know that my life would be very, very different had I not found my way to Christ.

Had it not been for the Savior of both our souls, my husband of twenty-four years and I would not still be married, and I would never have the kind of relationship that I have with our two incredible sons.

I grew up in a fairly affluent home, the third of four children. My mother and father were both from the Midwest and had met in high school. My mother was a Jew, and her father and family vigorously fought the marriage. They married anyway, but my father agreed to raise the children as Jews. I spent most of my years, until about age twelve, in the synagogue and celebrated all the traditional holidays with our Jewish relatives.

In reality, I grew up in a godless home, with no spiritual guidance or direction. Although my father had an extremely successful career and saw a great deal of financial success from it, our family became more and more dysfunctional as both my parents began drinking. My mother fell into a depression for which she had to be hospitalized several times. I was my mother's baby, and I did not understand.

My father traveled frequently for his job, and many of his trips took him out of the country for weeks at a time. So during all of this, he was either not home, at the office, or at home drinking. My father could be harsh, critical, and at times verbally abusive. My older brother and sister, I believe, suffered more from his abuse than my little brother or I, and they handled these dysfunctions in their own ways.

My brother rebelled and ran away from home at sixteen years old, and my sister buried herself in an obsession over dance and maintaining a dancer's body. This led to years and years of serious eating disorders and emotional illness. At fourteen, she left home for stays in mental hospitals and later to live with relatives out of state until she finished high school.

Shortly after my baby brother was born (I was eight), my mother was diagnosed with breast cancer, and we found out that my father had a girlfriend. He shortly thereafter divorced my mom, moved out, and married his girlfriend. As my mother became sicker from the radiation and chemo treatments, I remember spending a lot of time with friends, relatives, and housekeepers, and finding myself in the role of mother to my young brother. I carried huge amounts of responsibility and emotional burden for a young preteen girl. During that time I developed a lot of anger and bitterness toward my father for what I perceived he had done to my mother, and that certainly did not improve when we lost my mother to her breast cancer battle.

I remember as vividly as if it were yesterday the memory of being called out of my eighth-grade class at school for my father to pick me up. I knew as I walked out of that school and saw him, standing there by his car waiting for me, that my mother was gone—my only friend, ally, confidant, dead of cancer at forty-two years old. I was twelve, and my baby brother was only four.

My feelings of loneliness and despair were over-whelming at times. My brother and I had to go live with my father and stepmother, whom I greatly resented. She was a good woman, with good intentions, and to her credit, she really tried, but she also was not really interested in being a mother. Likewise, I was not interested in allowing anyone to replace the mother I'd lost.

Over the remainder of my childhood, I attended churches from time to time with various friends. On several occasions, I heard critical and prejudicial remarks regarding Jews, which left me very uncomfortable and at times angry toward the church, Christianity, and God.

I remember asking my maternal grandmother and my aunt about Jesus, and why our religion was different from the Christians. I actually would receive answers like, "Oh, honey, it is not that big a deal. The only difference is they believe Jesus is God's Son, and we don't." (As if that were no big thing.) I now realize that they knew no better themselves.

I struggled spiritually and emotionally for my entire life, knowing something was missing in my life but not knowing what. Then, a few years ago, my husband and I began attending church services on the Sundays that we had business conferences with another team we were working with. Many of those weekends I would make an excuse not to attend the service, as all of our business partners there were Christians. All the while, I was still angry and resentful that they expected me to attend.

I understand now that those agonizing times, alone in the hotel room, refusing to go to the service with my husband, was Satan at work. A Jew becoming a believer is probably one of Satan's biggest blows, and I'm sure he will fight as hard as he can to prevent it from happening. For a long time, I allowed myself to be controlled by it, by him.

In one of these Sunday services, in 2005, my husband rededicated his life to Christ. From the moment he did, his life was changed in some very significant ways. He had spent years and years denying addictions to alcohol and drugs that were ruining his health, not to mention our relationship. But watching him totally walk away from those things after he let Jesus into his heart, I began softening and finding myself thanking God for the incredible changes I was seeing in my husband. I still felt torn and conflicted—Satan was fighting harder!

Then my husband announced to me that he was going to take the boys and start attending church, which he did—without me. After attending this church a few times, putting no pressure on me, he came home one Sunday and said, "You know, the pastor of this church has an amazing outlook and heart for the Jews. I know after all your bad experiences, this might be hard for you to believe, but you need to come see for yourself."

I attended this church's service with my family the next Sunday, probably more out of curiosity than anything else. "Could there really be a Christian church that spoke well of the Jews?" I thought. That Sunday I heard a message from this amazing pastor that spoke to my heart and spoke of the direction of their ministry's passion for the Jews and for Israel. I had never seen this in a church before, and I knew then that God had brought me to this church for a reason. I continued to struggle with my feelings that I would be betraying my Jewish heritage by accepting Christ, but I also knew I needed to be there.

A few months later I experienced the first time that I could truly say that God had spoken to me. I felt as if I were getting to my feet through no volition of my own as I heard His soft voice tell me, "Linda, it's time for you to accept Me." It was, without a doubt, the most incredible thing that has ever happened in my life. Since that morning of salvation, I have seen my life change for the better in so many ways.

Another time in this initial journey, God spoke to me again on something that set me free. You see, as I accepted Christ and began to study the New Testament and His teachings, I began to agonize over where my mother was. I could not accept that she was not in heaven. Then one weekend at a women's conference, my tears began to flow. I found myself on my knees thinking about nothing but the loss of my mother and crying out to God, "Where is she?" Suddenly my anguish disappeared, a calm came over me, and again I heard this beautiful voice say, "Be still. She is with me." I know I will see my mother again.

At this point in my journey, I just long to find more and more time in my life to study and worship and understand how to better enhance my walk with the Lord. I continue to seek from Him what He is calling me to do as I continue to pray that my life and my story will help others to understand His salvation. Many are confused when I share that I am a Jew and a Christian, but as my pastor's mother once gently explained, "Linda, don't you realize, you never stopped being a Jew. That is your heritage, and you are one of His chosen people. No, you are simply a Jew who knows her savior."

My prayer for you, dear friend, is that if you do not

know your Savior, you will open your heart to Jesus and let His plans become your hope and future.

{ STRANDS of HOPE }

· ·

For God so loved the world that he gave his
one and only Son, that whoever believes in
him shall not perish but have eternal life.

–JOHN 3:16

· ·

God loved us so much that He sent His only son to die for us. As incredible as it sounds, salvation is a gift from God. We don't deserve it, and we sure can't earn it. It must be received as a gift.

John the Baptist made it very clear that people have only two choices when it comes to making a decision about Christ. Those who believe will have everlasting life, and those who do not believe will be rejected and face the wrath of God. There is no middle ground.

The invitation to accept Christ is clear. Romans 10:13 says, "Everyone who calls on the name of the Lord will be saved." Salvation happens when we confess to being a sinner, repent of it, and ask Christ to take control of our lives.

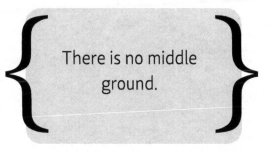

There is no middle ground.

If you have never asked Jesus Christ to be your personal Savior, you can ask Him right now. In fact, you can pray something like this:

Dear God, thank You for loving me so much that You sent Your Son to die for my sins. I admit that I need Your love and forgiveness. I believe that Jesus paid for my sins on the cross, and I receive Him by faith as my personal Savior. I accept the free gift of salvation as my very own.

Think About It

- Have you ever asked yourself, "Why would anyone die for me?"

- Have you ever loved anyone enough to die for them?

- How is love measured in John 15:13?

- As human beings, we share a need to be loved, and God wants us to love each other. In what ways can we show love to others?

- Share your salvation experience! Where were you when "God called"?

Pray About It

All-knowing heavenly Father, thank You for
accepting me just the way I am.

Cultivate a confidence in me that relies
on Your abilities and not my own. Your
strength is made perfect in my weakness.

Cover me with the feathers of Your wing, and
let me find rest in the shadow of the cross.

Evangelize my home or wherever I may go by
the power of Your Word lived out in my life.

Place a hedge of protection around me, O
Lord. Be my forward and my rear guard.

Teach me to place no other gods before You.

Enable me to serve You without fear, in holi-
ness and righteousness all the days of my life.

Drive me into Your arms daily, so that we
never lose our intimacy.

Amen

Chapter 8

Secrets of the Single

W hen we begin on any new trip there is always a little anticipation about how far it is, what you'll do when you get there, and if you can actually find the way. I don't believe it's any different when our lives have been shattered and have fallen apart around us. We still ask these same questions! Beginning a new life, without a man, was something I had never experienced.

I knew that I was beginning to embark on a journey like I had never been on before. My heavenly Father was asking me to step out of the boat and walk with Him, hand in hand. And I was reminded, "Faith is being sure of what we hope for and certain of what we do not see" (Hebrews 11:1).

As I prayed throughout the day, I felt help was on the way. I remember telling God how lonesome I was. Then, as He filled my spirit with hope, He let me know that there were many others out there experiencing the same feelings. Instead of sitting around feeling sorry for myself, I decided to do something about it. What's the most logical thing I could do? Invite those people to join me on my journey. And that's exactly what I did!

> **Instead of sitting around feeling sorry for myself, I decided to do something about it.**

I went to my pastor with the idea of starting a singles ministry. He assured me that I would have the support of the church. So, with lots of prayers and financial support, we began our journey. After any birthing process, naming the baby always seems to be the hardest. What would we call ourselves?

The Ryman in downtown Nashville, Tennessee, was a place I loved visiting. It is full of good old country music history. One weekend a group called Point of Grace was performing. When they sang a song called "Circle of Friends," I punched my friends and said, "That's the name of our new singles group!" God gave me the name, right there at the Grand Old Opry!

From the first time I heard this song, I knew it would mean something special to me and to this group God was forming. The song talked about how we were made to love and to be loved, and if we cry there will be friends to wipe our tears away. Having heard the powerful words of this song, we formed a group of Christian singles that were interested in the same goals. We wanted to explore new friendships, to learn how to be single and satisfied, and to have love and acceptance by a family where you are never alone. For years, everything I did was driven by my search for love. But now I was celebrating something I never knew was so important, "A Circle of Friends."

As my new friends filed through the doors of our first get-together, it became

{ The faces I saw needed to be happy and accepted again. }

obvious that we all had acquired several scars from this thing called life. I remember so well, as I greeted at the door, the facial expressions they wore. Some had smiles, but many had sadness. The faces I saw needed to be happy and accepted again. You know, the world would like for you to think it's only for couples. When you're single, you feel there is something wrong with you because you're alone. I remember I would never go to a restaurant alone because people would stare. So that's the very first thing Circle of Friends did. We decided we would go to different restaurants once or twice a month, to enjoy the fabulous food we had been missing. Yep, we gained a few pounds, but it was sure worth it.

We started having group meetings twice a month with guest speakers who taught us about saving money for retirement, facts about depression, music, beauty tips, and more. We even had a chili cook-off and a cake decorating contest. We went to Mr. Roy's farm for a cookout and hayride. It's amazing how much hugging goes on underneath a bunch of blankets on a cold night!

Circle of Friends was known for its hugs. We saw many folks who hadn't been hugged in years. Whatever your age, you can remember times throughout your life when a hug made you feel loved, worthwhile, comfortable, safe, welcome, and special. A hug is powerful. It's the act of closing your arms around someone and opening your heart to them. A hug has the power to heal broken relationships and mend wounded spirits. And a hug was something that as single people—no matter how independent—we couldn't do alone.

Wednesday, 10:00 a.m. – Ray

Ray is a successful banker who never meets a stranger. He's a handsome man and one heck of a dancer!

In September of 1996, I had a shock to my life and faith. I got a divorce that I didn't want. At fifty years old, I had been married for twenty-seven years and had two grown children. My wife said she wanted a divorce, and that was it—I had no choice but to give it to her. I kept the house and she moved out (sounds like a country song).

After that, I didn't know where to turn. We had been very active in church, but I really didn't want to go back and face all our church family. I felt the best thing to do was just not to go to church, to do other things on Sunday mornings, like sleep. I took this approach for several months, but my life seemed to have a hole in it. It wasn't full. Something was missing.

One Sunday night I was sitting at home watching TV and decided that I had been away from church long enough. I called our choir director and asked him if choir practice was still on Wednesday nights. This got me back into church, but still something was missing. Our church seemed to be all family-oriented. There wasn't much for a single person to do. It wasn't too long till I received a call from Cherie, talking about starting a singles group. We serve an on-time God!

There isn't anything better than having someone to talk to who has walked the same road you have. Circle of Friends was an outlet for many people, and we began to enjoy life with a renewed hope. Movies, picnics, hayrides, and canoeing trips gave us a new-found sense of belonging and worth. Our shared faith in Jesus Christ brought us together and kept us together.

To this day, the group is still going strong. Several people met and married someone through the Circle of Friends. Some used this group to get back on their feet so they could get on with their lives. I used this circle to help me get myself straightened out, and I met new people who are today good friends. Someone once told me that a man is lucky if he has one real

friend. I feel so fortunate that God lead me to Circle
of Friends.

Every Day, 5:00 p.m. – Jim

Starched shirts and creased slacks are two of the first things
you notice about Jim. His sweet spirit and beautiful smile
get attention from all the single ladies. Graying around the
temples is a fantastic look for this handsome guy.

Having come from a family where family values and
vows made before God were considered sacred, I was
not prepared for what was about to happen in my life.

In the spring of 1995, while on a trip to Los Angeles
with my wife of thirty years, she told me that she didn't
love me anymore and thought we should get a divorce.
We had two children, one in college and the other in
high school. My wife and I had our disagreements over
the years, but nothing serious enough to cause this type
of response. Thinking back, however, I had noticed she
had been growing quite cool toward me.

After our return home, everything seemed to go
along as usual for some time. There were times, of
course, when we would discuss why she felt the way

she did about our marriage, and all I could get from her was that we had just grown apart over the years. (That's the line they all say when they want to get rid of you.) After some six years of trying to work on our marriage, it became obvious to her that I was not going to initiate any divorce action, so she served me with divorce papers. She moved out, and the divorce was final in the spring of 2001. So here I was, sixty years old, divorced, and alone. I sold my home of twenty-eight years, kept very little furniture, and was commuting to work in a 1979 Ford truck. This was not a very good time in my life, to say the least.

After long days at work, it soon became a habit for those I worked with and myself to go out for dinner and drinks at a local restaurant. This had not been the norm for me since my college days many years ago. But one night I found myself reverting back to some of my old ways, drinking and driving. I realized quickly that this was a path I didn't want back on.

I enrolled in a Divorce Care class at the church I was attending, thinking maybe I could make some sense of all I was going through. The classes helped me to understand that God loved me no matter what had happened in my life and that His love was unconditional. Many times those who have experienced divorce tend to think that they are defective in some way and are somehow incapable of a normal relationship. The Divorce Care program enables one to overcome this feeling of guilt and emphasizes the need for one to forgive one's self as well as the other person. I had never stopped going to church during this whole mess, but somehow now it meant so much more to me. It was as if God had His arms around me and was protecting me from the pain of the world.

One Sunday I accepted an invitation from my daughter and her husband to attend their church on Friend Day. I accepted and was introduced to many friendly folks. I remember meeting the teacher of the singles class that day. She invited me to come to her class the next week. The next Sunday I attended the class and met a lot of singles, who seemed to be very content to be single. This was exactly the kind of group I had been searching for. I also started going to a monthly meeting called Circle of Friends. The group was made up of singles, both men and women, ranging from thirty to seventy-five. They were from the local area, as well as neighboring towns. My Sunday school teacher was the leader of that group as well. Once or twice a month the group would get together and eat out (I hate to eat alone) at a local restaurant, or we would have a guest speaker. It beat going to the local bars!

Meanwhile, I had noticed that the leader (my teacher) didn't seem to be attached to anyone in particular. So I made it a point to talk to her. She was a hairdresser with two children and had been single for seven years. I soon learned that she was just as beautiful on the inside as she was on the outside.

Well, to make a long story short, I married that beautiful lady and we are now in our ninth year of the most wonderful marriage I could ever hope for.

In the process of writing this book, she asked me to give my God story. She said she didn't want the story of how we met, but what God has done for me in my life. Well, I contend that they are one in the same, because if God had not led me to meet her that Sunday on Friend Day, I would have no story to tell.

{ STRANDS of HOPE }

Greater love has no one than this,
that he lay down his life for his friends.

–JOHN 15:13

Friendships have been treasured throughout the ages as one of God's greatest gifts. Friendship unites our emotions, binds our hearts, and melts two souls into one. True friendships are unwavering, whether they are cultivated across the backyard fence or across the miles.

Take a moment to value the friendships in your own life.

Think About It

- What makes a good friend?

- A friend makes _____.

- A friend keeps _____.

- A friend celebrates _____.

- A friend forgives _____.

Pray About It

Cover me with the feathers of Your wing,
Most High God. Hide me under the shadow
of the Almighty.

Oh how my soul rejoices in Your faithful
provision!

Nurture contentment within me; I never want
to be unhappy with what You have given me.

Teach me to bank Your promises in the vault
of my heart, so that I won't sin myself
bankrupt.

Each day let me rise and call You blessed, forgive my sins, and fill me with Your Spirit.

Nothing is too difficult for You, Lord.

Thank You for showing me compassion and
mercy. Do not let me stray from the course
You have set before me.

Amen

Chapter 9

Secrets of the Impatient

isten. . . . Can you hear it? It's the faint tinkling of music. A melody that you hear over and over again as you wait . . . and you wait . . . and you wait. You think it's never coming. Then all of a sudden, it rounds the curve, into your neighborhood, and you begin to explode with excitement!

As a child, one of my favorite things in the summertime was to visit my aunt. She lived in the city, so it was a treat to go to her house. All the neighborhood kids would gather when the sounds of that celebrated ice-cream truck would get closer. It was always worth the wait, when I could finally get my hands on that wonderful fudge popsicle. Ah, I can almost taste it now.

I hate to wait. I believe it is one of the most difficult things to do. It always seems like the more I want something, the harder it is to wait. Whether I am waiting for a taxi, a phone call, or maybe an answer to prayer, it's never easy.

> The more I want something, the harder it is to wait.

The Bible is full of stories where people had to wait. In Genesis 17, Abraham and Sarah had to wait, and in Genesis 30, Rachel and Jacob had to wait too. We need to remember that God's timing is different from ours. He sees things from a different perspective, because He understands the big picture.

As we deal with the pressures of daily living, one of the greatest challenges we face in life is that of mistaking our timing for God's timing. When a crisis arises, our natural human response is to take matters into our own hands and react accordingly, never giving any thought as to what God's plan may be. Learning to consult God *first* in these situations is most certainly a learned trait that requires much discipline on our part as Christ followers.

We have to look with confidence toward the journey He has for us, trusting that He will bring to pass the plan He has designed for you and me. In his book *God Will Always Be There for You*, Robert Moment gives us three actions that will help you to wait patiently and, with faith, help you to know and believe that God will be there to help:

Trust: Scripture tells us that God is unchangeable, which means He is the same yesterday, today, and tomorrow. We can depend on Him to lead us on the right path. We must trust in His plan!

Resist: We must resist the temptation to take matters into our own hands. The safest place we can rest is in God's will. When we rest here, resisting temptation is a lot easier.

Pray: How many times have we given a prayer request to God and felt like He was deaf? God always answers; it may not be the way we want or expect. During these times we have to keep on praying. It may be yes, no, or even something *better*.

One thing I have come to understand and believe is that

we don't even need to understand the question, if we know the One who has the answers.

Many times along this journey I have been asked, "How did you get to the place where you were willing to write this book and to speak to hundreds of women about God's healing and forgiveness?" Kicking and screaming, that's how! You see, I always thought I had to keep my secrets. I thought if I told anyone where I'd been and what I had done, no one would ever look at me the same. Yes, it requires courage, but each one of us has the same opportunity every day to be a witness of our Lord's healing love to a world of wounded hearts. Whether we like it or not, we are all God's ambassadors if we wear the name *Christian.*

> He's the only One who can take your "mess" and make it into "His Message."

My prayer is that every day you will become less broken and more loved as you experience the God who transforms lives from worthless into valuable, guilty into innocent, hungry into contented, and empty into full. In every situation you face, I want to encourage you to remember His grace, believe His truth, and seek His face. He's the only One who can take your "mess" and make it into "His Message."

Wednesday, 1:00 p.m. – Sara

Sara reminds me of a sweet little grandmother. She wears her hair in a shoulder-length bob, and I'm sure the gray that's showing is a result of many years of abuse, both mental and physical. Still, she maintains her sweet spirit and beautiful smile.

Mistake #1

My father was very authoritative. I wasn't allowed to wear jeans or makeup or date. The first time I married was just to get away from him. My husband was an alcoholic (as was his father). Jobs were hard to find or hold on to when his world revolved around alcohol. He tried to get me to drink with him, but I couldn't stand it. It got so bad that I had to get out of that marriage.

After lots of talking with God, He forgave me and gave me peace of mind. We had one daughter, and our split-up really hurt her. This still grieves me.

Mistake #2

Four years later I met a man who didn't smoke or drink and had a steady job. Praise the Lord! Since I didn't know what love was, when he asked me to marry him, I said yes.

Less than six months into the marriage, I was wondering, "What have I done?" But I was already pregnant, so I had no choice but to stay. My husband was the baby of his family, and he had his way regardless of anyone else's thoughts or feelings. You did things his way or paid the consequences. This made my life miserable. We had two daughters, and neither one of us would give them up, so I had to stay there until they left home. By then I was so depressed, I wanted to die. We divorced in 1997.

All during these thirty years I constantly prayed and talked to God. After one more failure, I thought, "Oh, God, why can't I learn to wait on You instead of choosing for myself?"

Mistake #3

Eight years later I thought God told me I would marry very soon. That was a shock because I wasn't seeing anyone. (I have later learned that Satan talks also.) Then I met a man, and our lives changed from first sight. We didn't know if it was love then (he still doesn't know), but we married anyway. After a couple of months he started having second thoughts. He became so distant that we split up and divorced. He has drifted further away, and now we seldom see each other. Friends tell me he constantly asks about me. (Why do they tell me that?)

Caring about him and wanting him to come back is killing me. The days are long and the nights are even longer.

Psalm 147:3 says, "He heals the brokenhearted and binds up their wounds."

I totally depend on Jesus every day to strengthen, comfort, and guide me. I can't do it on my own.

Wednesday, 10:30 a.m. – Don

As a seventh grader, Don's life's ambition was to be a toothpick manufacturer. What an imagination! With his dry wit and calm personality, followed by his amazing smile, anyone would be blessed to have him as a friend.

I have always loved the outdoors. It has always felt right to hold a fishing rod or a gun in my hand. I loved to stay with my grandparents in the summer, because they lived in the country. I didn't have any siblings until I was sixteen, and then along came a baby sister. I was spoiled rotten.

My parents were supportive in everything I did. Dad always came to my games, but I never was able to communicate with him much. Mom was so different— she was the fun one. Everyone always wanted to come over to my house to play.

When I found out they were getting a divorce, after twenty-four years of marriage, I was a little shocked. Unfortunately, not as shocked as my father was to find out she had been unfaithful to him.

After high school I went to college, and I hated it. I wanted to go to a trade school, but I did what my mom asked me to do. I partied too much, which resulted in my exiting college and entering the Marine Corps in 1969. When I stepped foot on the bus to go to camp, my life immediately started to change. The Marine Corps was terribly hard. The beatings were brutal. There were times I thought I was going to die, and wished I could. They would break you down to build you up into the man they wanted you to be. The goal was to weed out the weak ones and make warriors out of the strong ones. In 1972, I went to Vietnam with ten thousand other young men. We learned to hate our fellow man and not to trust anyone. Someone asked me if I prayed while I was in Vietnam, and I told them when you have bombs going off all around your head, you tend to talk to the man upstairs. I wasn't sure who that was, though, because I never had any relationship with God. I did my tour of duty in Vietnam for one year and served in the Marines for four years. I entered the Marines weighing over two hundred pounds and came home at one hundred forty-two pounds.

What was the first thing I did when I touched the fertile soil of the United States? I got drunk! That's right: I had become a full-fledged alcoholic. All we did over there was fight and drink. Now all I wanted to do was just kill the pain. Most of the years after my returning home are still a blur, because I drank all day, every day.

Relationships didn't go well for me either. With a baby girl and two failed marriages under my belt, I believed that love was not in my future until I met and married my soul mate on October 18, 2004. She brought out something in me that I never believed I had: the ability to love and trust someone again. Shortly after we married, I was diagnosed with IPF, Idopathic Pulmonary Fibrosis. I knew nothing about this disease, but I knew the prognosis was not good.

We had begun to go to church and God was beginning to speak to me again during this time of uncertainty in my life. When someone tells you that you're going to die, it makes you take a hard look at your life. Did I want to take a chance of dying and not going to heaven, or did I want to be a believer and go to heaven? I had not made many good choices in my life, but this one was a no-brainer. I received Christ as my personal savior in April of 2005 at a revival held at our church. After that decision, my whole attitude changed. The things I used to do and say were no longer desirable. Death didn't scare me anymore.

Everyone has a Goliath in their life, and you have to face it. I have a "rock" that signifies my fight that I knew I was going to be up against.

On my way to church one morning, we received the call: "Get your clothes together, and meet us at the airport in one hour. We have new lungs for you." I received my double lung transplant at Duke University Hospital on November 12, 2006. We stayed there for four months. When I returned home, God opened doors for me to share my testimony and speak firsthand on the importance of being an organ donor.

I hope I have shared my love for Christ to all those who have crossed my path. "Godly" is not something we simply decide to be. It is the description of a person who truly follows Jesus so closely that he or she becomes more like Him, bringing blessings and words that draw others to Christ.

Life's uncertainties sometimes center our attention on the problems instead of on God, and we forget He said, "Take no thought for tomorrow." When I am in the middle of a mess, I have tunnel vision that focuses on my problem. I have to discipline my thoughts to concentrate on the truths of God's Word.

Well, on February 9, 2009, I was hit with another of life's challenges. Three years after my transplant, I started experiencing rejection from RSV pneumonia. All my days of playing golf, a sport I dearly love, had come to a halt. My doctors told me that my only chance for survival was another lung transplant. We learned that the survival rate for re-transplants was not high. We started on our search for a hospital that would actually take us, because my age and other factors were against me. Back to the doctors, back to the hospitals, back to the IVs, and back to not breathing well.

When I stop and think about it, probably the worst thing we can do to God is to want something more than we want Him. When that happens, we begin worshipping an idol instead of the Creator who loves us so much.

My body was beginning to die again. Slowly my life and breath were fading away. But was it my life or God's? He had already given me new life in Him and a new set of lungs. What else did I need? Well, the doctors were telling me what I needed was another set of lungs to survive again. "Survive again?" I thought. Then I remembered my "Rock" and "The Fight." Death no longer had a hold over me. If God was ready for me to come home, well, I was ready, but if He wasn't, I had one more fight in me.

Surviving many months of preparation and waiting in anticipation for another chance to breathe normally again, I drew closer to my Maker. My body was beginning to shrink in weight and muscle. Talk about a weight loss plan! Time was running out!

I clearly remember the last trip to Vanderbilt, in the back of the ambulance. I wondered if this was it, the last time I would see my wife, or maybe my last day on this earth. Jeremiah 29:11 tells us, "'For I know the plans I have for you,' declares the LORD, 'plans to prosper you and not to harm you, plans to give you hope and a future.'" Well, He had done a good job so far. I believed I was in good hands. Whatever the outcome was, I was a winner.

{ STRANDS of HOPE }

. . . .

But those who wait on the LORD
Shall renew their strength;
They shall mount up with wings like eagles,
They shall run and not be weary,
They shall walk and not faint.

–ISAIAH 40:31 NKJV

. . . .

Quietly waiting on God encourages us more to restore our bodies, minds, and emotions than anything else we can do. Do you ever have times when you get upset, worried, and anxious? I encourage you to spend quiet time with God.

During these times alone with Him, He will empower you to face everything you need to accomplish, with renewed mental, physical, and spiritual strength.

If you are struggling in your life right now, come and take a seat at Jesus' feet. Rest in His presence.

Think About It

- Have you ever felt as though you were in God's presence? What did you experience?

- Tell of a situation where you had to wait on something. Was it worth waiting for?

- Explain how waiting on something renews your strength.

- How does sitting at Jesus feet satisfy your soul?

Pray About It

Great and awesome Creator, You made me according to Your perfect design. I am honored to bear Your image.

Replace any lies that the enemy may have told me with Your truth.

Apply the blood of Jesus to the doorposts of my heart, and make me clean.

Thank You for the plans You have designed for my life. I know Your plans are to prosper me and not to harm me.

Enable me to trust in Your plans. I know You plan to give me hope and a future.

Fulfill Your good and perfect purpose in my life as I submit myself into Your capable hands.

Untie the strings of disobedience that bind me to my sin, and set me free.

Let me clearly see Your active presence in my life, and give me a grateful heart.

Amen

Chapter 10

Secrets of the Forgiven

We all have some sort of big secret, don't we? When we refuse to face that secret, it can often become a lifelong tap dance, constantly trying to keep it hidden and cover up any consequences that came along with it. If we don't deal with the reality of its effects and reach a state of true forgiveness and healing, that shame can influence our lives forever.

By now you know that I've had a *lot* of secrets. The only way I could stop dwelling on my secretive past and get on with my God-given future was to come to terms with my secrets, once and for all. Although I had a lot to choose from, the secret that seemed to haunt me the most was my choice to have an abortion. Through the loving counsel of dear friends, I finally found a way to deal with that secret, allowing the forgiveness and grace of God to bring that secret out of the dark and into the healing light of His love.

Grieving is a normal and healthy response to a major loss through death. This painful process helps relieve our sorrow and grief. However, after an abortion, women may attempt to bury their grief, turn their emotions off, and even run from God. But in order to experience complete healing, we must first face the fact that abortion ended the lives of our unborn babies.

Like most of us do, I maintained focus on the things that I enjoyed in life and put off the things that made me sad. I had lived in denial for years about making the decision to end my child's life.

> I had lived in denial for years about making the decision to end my child's life.

But undeniably, when the subject came up and questions were asked, an emotional response was triggered within me that forced me to face my feelings about the "truth" of abortion. I had never taken full responsibility for my baby's death. I had hidden behind the idea that abortion was my only answer.

My dear friends Joanne and Pam saw me struggling with my past and encouraged me to go through a post-abortion Bible study for women. Many times in the hair salon we would talk about the necessary emotional healing, and soon I realized that this was something that I needed to do. I joined an eight-week study, called Forgiven and Set Free, at the pregnancy counseling clinic.

In the weeks and months of the Bible study, I was taught about the character of God and about His love and forgiveness. Can you say "I am forgiven" with confidence? Psalm 103 is full of assurances that He loves you and me. Also, in this study, we learn where our babies are now and whether we will recognize them in heaven.

One of the most powerful exercises I did was for the purpose of bringing my grief into focus, releasing my emotions, and giving my child a name. God had already showed me through a dream that my child was a little girl. If anyone's child had been born, he or she would have been given a name. I so much wanted to restore some sort of dignity to the broken image of this unborn child, so I gave her the name Claire Ann.

At the close of the study, my family and a few friends

attended a small, intimate memorial service for Claire Ann. I was asked to write a letter to my daughter, and I include it here to share with you.

Dearest Child,

After twenty-six years, I can't believe I am writing this letter to you. When I found out I was carrying you inside me, I made the only decision I thought at the time was available. I went to the hospital and had a doctor perform a D&C, then left there never considering that I had given the orders to end your life. I am so sorry; it was one of the biggest mistakes of my life.

Many years later you came to me several times in my sleep, crying out, "Mommy." I remember so well the night I saw you looking in my bedroom window. You were a beautiful, blonde-haired, little girl. You looked just like a little angel. Since that time, I knew it was God's way of letting me know that I had given birth to a little girl and that He was taking care of you.

I have given you the name Claire Ann. Ann is my middle name and this is my way of always keeping you as a part of me. I believe that you and God have forgiven me, and I am looking forward to the day when I can hold you in my arms, just like I held your brother and sister.

Good-bye for now, my precious daughter.

Certificate of Life

Whereas, on or about the fourteenth day of May, 1982, a baby was expected to be born of
Cherie Gipson Jobe, his natural mother.

Whereas, this child went to be with Jesus before birth.

Be it known, the undersigned acknowledge the worth and dignity due the child called by his mother

Claire Ann

and who is acknowledged by this mother as a full member of her family and a creation equal with all other human beings created in the image of God, having the same inherent and immeasurable value.

*This child lives eternally with Jesus
and in the heart and mind of his mother, now and forever.*

DANNY GIPSON

Jim Jobe
Witnesses

Cherie Gipson Jobe
Mother of this Child

That time of mourning and remembrance for my little Claire Ann not only put my shameful secret out in the open, but it also allowed me to share it with those most precious to me, while accepting their forgiveness at the same time.

> { Healing certainly doesn't render us perfect, but it does allow us to move on. }

It gave me time to focus on forgiving myself and to truly

understand that God had forgiven me the very first time I had asked. Only with forgiveness can the healing begin.

Healing certainly doesn't render us perfect, but it does allow us to move on and, if we choose, help others who haven't yet received healing and forgiveness from their own secret wounds.

Wednesday, 10:30 a.m. – Hannah

"Beautiful inside and out" is a perfect description of Hannah. She has that natural glow that says she should be in a Dove commercial. She wears very little makeup, and her hair has the most beautiful sun-glittering highlights. Hannah and I both understand the shame of secrets—and the power of forgiveness.

Born in 1971 in Nashville, Tennessee, I was adopted at two months of age. My childhood was fairly normal in a middle-class family with a great mom and dad who supported me in everything I did, including competitive skating and dance. But my heart always longed to be a teacher.

My life took a tragic turn at age seventeen or eighteen; I can't tell you exactly when, because I've blocked it out. I remember taking the pregnancy test at my boyfriend's house. He was the father and the guy I would later marry. When the test came back positive, I remember having the most disgusting and shameful feeling in the pit of my stomach. I couldn't tell my dad.

Shortly after taking the test, I did tell my mother. My boyfriend did not encourage me to abort the baby; it was my mother who said, "We must take care of this situation." I have no idea how she found the clinic, but I still clearly recall that day. As I sat on the bed, the nurse asked me if I wanted to do this, and I said no. Then I woke up, and it was all over. We didn't talk about it on the way home and never have spoken of it again.

I have chosen to tell my story because of 2 Corinthians 1:3–5. It tells us that God never wastes a wound because our pain gives us the ability to empathize with others who have suffered and walked down the same paths we have. Through the comforting power of God, we are able to come alongside those who have experienced our same pain and know exactly what they need. When facing any difficulty, we have to trust God and rest in His compassionate and loving arms.

A question was asked one Sunday in my Bible class, "If time or money was no issue, what would you like to do for God?" To my amazement, I blurted out, "I would like to work with young women who have a crisis pregnancy going on." I had no idea where that answer came from, but soon a person at my church connected me with the Pregnancy Support Center. I thought I'd go in there and "save the world" by helping everyone who had been adopted or who had been through an abortion.

When I began helping at the clinic, I remember a question they asked me, "Have you ever had an abortion?" What would I do? Nobody, except my mother and the baby's father, knew. But I couldn't lie! The staff at the center needed to know "where I was" before I could volunteer to help others.

As I shared my story, I remember being like a stammering idiot. I couldn't believe I was acting this way. I knew in my head that God had forgiven me, but it seemed I didn't believe in my heart that He really would. As a result of that meeting, they suggested I attend a post-abortion class.

As a child I pictured God to be someone we prayed

to and went to heaven to be with if we were good enough. I remember more of the Bible stories than I remember about who God is. "Good enough" was something I never thought I could be.

As a result of the post-abortion study, God is now real! He is the only thing I have. As small as I am, a bleep on His radar, He listens to me. His word is for me. Before, my relationship with God was a wall. I felt so much shame; I couldn't get over it. Now I realize that we have a free gift of forgiveness from Him. We can accept it or not. He lives inside of me. I now have peace.

I believe women have difficulty receiving God's love after an abortion because Satan doesn't want you to know that God offers forgiveness. He wants you to believe that you have committed a sin that will bring you shame for the rest of your life. Don't buy into that lie! Second Corinthians 5:17 says, "If anyone is in Christ, he is a new creation; the old has gone, the new has come!"

The study also taught me that I could celebrate my child's life. In my quiet time with God, I could see my baby boy in God's hands. He was with Jesus; he was laughing. My quiet time is so important. When the memories of the abortion sometime return, I find that

143

staying in God's Word reminds me of how much He loves me.

When the State of Tennessee opened adoption laws, I wrote a letter requesting to find my real parents. It took about a year and a half, but I found them. The social worker documented many little details that meant so much to me. My birth occurred in the Florence Crittenden Home for girls. My mother had gotten a little shawl set for me, and after my birth she wanted to see me one more time. The file said that she sat with me for a long time and gave me that shawl before leaving. I know now that she felt she was doing the best thing for me. It took a lot of courage to do that.

Today I counseled a thirteen-year-old who is pregnant. Another girl came in today who is "abortion minded." I told her, "You cannot see past your current crisis, but that part will go away. The pain of the abortion will never go away." I can now trust God with anything, no matter how big or small, and I know God has a purpose for my life.

[STRANDS of HOPE]

. . . .

Do not fear, for you will not be ashamed; Neither be disgraced, for you will not be put to shame; For you will forget the shame of your youth, And will not remember the reproach of your widowhood anymore.

–ISAIAH 54:4 NKJV

. . . .

Are your secrets still rooted in shame? You can be free from that shame through the power of Jesus Christ. In Isaiah 54:4, He has promised to remove shame. And in Isaiah 61:7, He promised to pour out a twofold blessing. We will possess double what we lost, and will have joy everlasting.

Think About It

- Are you able now to trust God with your hurt and shame caused by your secrets?

- What are some of the reasons women have difficulty with God's love and forgiveness?

- When I was a child I pictured God to be

  _____.

- What promises does God give us about relief from shame?
  Psalm 25:3
  Psalm 34:4–5
  Isaiah 54:4–8

- Share your secret now—either with God, your spouse, a trusted friend, or a member of your church family. Find comfort in knowing there is no shame.

Pray About It

Faithful and loving Father, thank You for loving
me enough to send Jesus to die in my place.

Occupy the deep recesses of my heart, and
turn me from darkness to light.

Renew my mind day after day, so that I may
see and recognize truth.

Guard my heart and my mind, and set my eyes
like a flint toward the cross of Jesus Christ.

I want to be loving and forgiving, just as in Christ
I have received grace and mercy in abundance.

Vault me up out of the mud and mire of my
sin, and help me to overcome my unbelief.

Enhance my knowledge of Your Word; I want to
wield it like a strong sword against my enemy.

Nothing compares to the peace I find in fel-
lowship with You, Almighty God.

Amen

Looking for Answers?

How to Become a Christian

The central theme of the Bible is God's love for you and for all people. This love was revealed when Jesus Christ, the Son of God, came into the world as a human being, lived a sinless life, died on the cross, and rose from the dead. Because Christ died, your sins can be forgiven, and because He conquered the grave, you can have eternal life.

The gospel is the "Good News" that because of what Christ has done, we can be forgiven and live forever.

But this gift of forgiveness and eternal life cannot be yours unless you accept it. God requires an individual response from you. The following verses from the Bible show God's part and yours in this process:

God's Love Is Revealed in the Bible

"For God so loved the world that he gave his only Son, that

whoever believes in him shall not perish but have eternal life." John 3:16

God loves you. He wants to bless your life and make it full and complete.

We Are Sinful

"For all have sinned and fall short of the glory of God." Romans 3:23

You may have heard someone say, "I'm only human; nobody's perfect." This Bible verse says the same thing: we are all sinners. We all do things that we know are wrong. And that's why we feel estranged from God—because God is holy and good, and we are not.

Christ Has Paid Our Penalty!

"But God demonstrates his own love for us in this: While we were still sinners, Christ died for us." Romans 5:8

The Bible teaches that Jesus Christ, the sinless Son of God, has paid the penalty for all your sins. You may think you have to lead a good life and do good deeds before God will love you. But the Bible says that Christ loved you enough to die for you, even when you were rebelling against Him.

Salvation Is a Free Gift

"For it is by grace you have been saved, through faith—and this not from yourselves, it is the gift of God—not by works, so that no one can boast." Ephesians 2:8–9

The word *grace* means "undeserved favor." It means God is offering you something you could never provide for yourself. God's gift of salvation is free. You do not have to work for it. All you have to do is joyfully receive it. Believe with all your heart that Jesus died for you!

You Must Receive Him

"Yet to all who received him, to those who believed in his name, he gave the right to become children of God." John 1:12

When you receive Christ into your heart, you become a child of God and have the privilege of talking to Him in prayer at any time about anything. The Christian life is a personal relationship with God through Jesus Christ. And best of all, it is a relationship that will last for all eternity.

If you make a commitment to Christ today, please let me know, so I can personally pray for you. Also, if you have a God story you would like to share, e-mail me at cheriejobeministry@gmail.com.

Truth Cards

On the following pages, I've included the scriptures from the Strands of Hope sections, plus I've added a couple of others that keep me going through the bad hair days of life.

Give these truths a trim, and carry them with your compact. Read them whenever your inner beauty needs a touch-up.

"Give thanks to the LORD, for he is good; his love endures forever." **Psalm 107:1**

— — — — — — — — — — — — — — —

"Therefore, if anyone is in Christ, he is a new creation; old things have passed away; behold, all things have become new." **2 Corinthians 5:17 NKJV**

— — — — — — — — — — — — — — —

"Peace I leave with you, My peace I give to you; not as the world gives do I give to you. Let not your heart be troubled, neither let it be afraid." **John 14:27 NKJV**

— — — — — — — — — — — — — — —

"Praise be to the God and Father of our Lord Jesus Christ, the Father of compassion and the God of all comfort, who comforts us in all our troubles, so that we can comfort those in any trouble with the comfort we ourselves have received from God." **2 Corinthians 1:3-4**

— — — — — — — — — — — — — — —

"Love the LORD your God with all your heart and with all your soul and with all your strength." **Deuteronomy 6:5**

— — — — — — — — — — — — — — —

"To everything there is a season, A time for every purpose under heaven." **Ecclesiastes 3:1 NKJV**

"For God so loved the world that he gave his one and only Son, that whoever believes in him shall not perish but have eternal life." **John 3:16**

— — — — — — — — — — — — — —

"Greater love has no one than this, that he lay down his life for his friends." **John 15:13**

— — — — — — — — — — — — — —

"But those who wait on the LORD, Shall renew their strength; They shall mount up with wings like eagles, They shall run and not be weary, They shall walk and not faint."
Isaiah 40:31 NKJV

— — — — — — — — — — — — — —

"Do not fear, for you will not be ashamed; Neither be disgraced, for you will not be put to shame; For you will forget the shame of your youth, And will not remember the reproach of your widowhood anymore." **Isaiah 54:4 NKJV**

— — — — — — — — — — — — — —

"If we ask anything according to His will, He hears us."
I John 5:14–15

— — — — — — — — — — — — — —

"I can do all things through Christ who strengthens me."
Philippians 4:13 NKJV

Acknowledgments

This book has truly been a team effort. I will forever be indebted to the many friends and colleagues who have labored and prayed with me about the direction of this book. I offer special gratitude to:

My secret sharers: Thanks so much for allowing readers to see straight into your heart—secrets and all!

The Kitchen Table Team: Karen Thrasher, Barbara Thomas, Monty Thomas, and Beth Thomas. What a joy it is to have friends like you in my life! You guys were the first to catch the vision for this book. Without your encouragement and friendship, this book may have never been birthed. Each one of you has used your own special gifts to give life to this project. I love each one of you!

Leslie Stephens: My deepest appreciation to you for your contribution to this book. Your gift of writing prayers is one few people have. Thanks so much for sharing it with my readers. (For any of my readers who would like to have a personalized prayer written for someone you love, you can go to Leslie's website: prayersforthepeopleyoulove.com.)

My editor: Thank you, Amy Parker! Our gifts are so different, but our love for our Lord is the same. Your careful and gifted editorial work is amazing!

My designer, Brecca Theele: I love your creativity and sense of style. I will be forever grateful for your patience in designing this awesome book cover!

Hair salon clients: Thousands of you have traveled this journey with me for over thirty years. Words cannot express my appreciation for your loyalty, patience, and friendship. It has been a "shear" pleasure to serve you!

To my two amazing children, Chandra and Danny: From the first time I held you both in my arms I felt loved. Your tolerance, love, and encouragement have carried me through the hard times. My heart is with you every day.

To my husband, Jim: You are sunshine to my heart! What I feel for you is a deep, total, and enduring love—that I can always count on. Thanks so much for encouraging me to take this challenge that God has set before me. I know you will always walk beside me, loving me with all your heart. And for that, I praise God for you!

Finally, my Savior, Jesus Christ: I haven't always understood why You chose me to share my story, but I hope this humble effort pleases You and brings glory to Your name. Thank You for restoring the broken places of my life and transforming me into a display of Your handiwork. I will forever be grateful for Your gift of unconditional love and grace.

About the Author

As an unwanted child, an abused wife, and a single mother, Cherie Jobe tried to compensate with the various lies that promised to fill the emptiness, but found that, in reality, these lies take women lower and lower into depression and feelings of worthlessness. When Cherie was willing to make radical choices, the result was a brand-new confidence and a freedom to be who God had designed her to be.

Now a happily married wife and doting mother, Cherie has served in ministry director positions in churches and traveled all over the country sharing her story and the wisdom she's gained through an imperfect life. As a speaker and author, Cherie's friendly smile, honest transparency, and genuine love for women—along with her Tennessee twang—endear her to audiences wherever she goes. She speaks to thousands of women annually, encouraging, giving hope, and helping each woman to come to terms with her own life's secrets.

Secrets from Behind the Chair can be used as curriculum for women's retreats and seminars. Cherie is available to appear at these events.

WWW.CHERIEJOBE.COM

Made in the USA
Charleston, SC
04 April 2015